WARNING!

PARENTAL DISCRETION ADVISED

Some of the illustrations contained in this book are *intense* and *provocative* and may promote *violence, occultism,* and *sexual promiscuity.* The amazing fact is that these illustrations came from comic books, library books, magazines, music albums, movies, and videos *readily available and designed expressly for children.* They are openly accessible to children at your local supermarket, public or school library, record store, and movie theatre, and come directly into your home by television. *Those in charge of Satan's New Age Plan will stop at nothing to destroy our kids!*

RAVAGED BY THE NEW AGE

*Satan's Plan
to Destroy Our Kids*

TEXE MARRS

LTP Living Truth Publishers
8103 Shiloh Court • Austin, Texas 78745

Scripture quotations are from the King James Version of
The Holy Bible.

Cover design: Britt Taylor Collins

Second printing, 1989

Printed in the United States of America

Library of Congress Catalog Card Number 88-083897

ISBN 0-9620086-1-3

ACKNOWLEDGEMENTS

Wanda and I express our sincerest thanks and appreciation to the dedicated members of our staff at Living Truth Ministries and the Association to Rescue Kids (ARK): Karen Chisholm, Cathy Maroney, Debra Pulliam and Cindy Rich. Their efforts on behalf of this book were substantial, and we praise God for the important part they are playing in bringing the Truth to so many. Also, we thank Paul Vick for his inspired work as Outreach Director of ARK and acknowledge the outstanding contribution of Lin Harris who so graciously volunteered her time and expertise to train our staff in desktop publishing so this book could be produced.

Our heartfelt appreciation also goes to the many wonderful and caring Christian men and women who have written to encourage us and have sent materials and information for our use in researching this important book.

Finally, and most importantly, we dedicate *RAVAGED BY THE NEW AGE* to our Lord Jesus Christ who called me to write this book. Our ministry is a living testimony that God's Word is fulfilled in the lives of those who trust Him:

I know thy works: behold, I have set before thee an open door, and no man can shut it. (Rev. 3:8)

T A B L E   O F
Contents

Preface

Satan has a Secret Plan to destroy our kids. The Lord of Hell wants our children, and he's determined to have them. Almost four decades ago, New Age leaders were given their marching orders by their hellish master. "Go forth," they were commanded, "and cast your rotten nets. Now is the time to harvest the youth of America and the globe."

It's time we tear off the Satanic mask of deception and lies. We must blow the lid off the conspiracy to steal our kids and protect them from horrendous assault by the New Age child abusers.

This is the first book to completely expose the New Age destruction of our children. Satan would like to keep his grotesque plans and activities underground. One top New Age figure has even boasted that the New Age Secret Plan is "occultly guarded." But that's not God's way. The Bible teaches that there is nothing hid that will not be uncovered. God wants His people to know the Truth.

RAVAGED BY THE NEW AGE exposes the awful truth about the New Age Plan of destruction. It reveals the dangerous, hidden messages in kids' TV shows, cartoons, toys, movies, comic books and books. It lays bare the cruel plan of New Age educators to seduce our children in the classroom, and names the major New Age cults that seek to lure our youth into captivity. And it chronicles the astonishing, hideous rise of devil worship, Satanism, and witchcraft among our youth. *This book is*

*must reading for every Christian leader, pastor, grand-
parent, and parent in America and the entire world!*

God has called me to reveal the grisly success that
Satan's New Age is experiencing in capturing the very
souls of our children. It must grieve our Heavenly Father
deeply to see what is now happening here below. Satan
has targeted for destruction the most vulnerable and
defenseless segment of humanity: the child.

Be forewarned: this book will change your life! The astonishing evidence it presents will leave you, as it did me,
in tears, heavy in spirit and burdened with cares for the
children who are being harmed. Anyone who strives to
live in the will of God has a soft spot in their hearts for
kids. To realize that harmless and sweet little boys and
girls and impressionable young teenagers are being hurt
and spiritually crippled by the Adversary is almost more
than a Christ-filled adult can bear.

The Bible tells us that children are very dear and
precious to Jesus. Lovingly embracing little children,
Christ told His disciples to care for little ones and not to
forbid them to seek after Him, "for of such is the kingdom
of heaven" (Matt. 19:14).

The New Age is evil and malignant far beyond what
we can imagine. We need to be aware of its magnitude
and fight its encroachments on our kids. But keep this
foremost in mind: *your children do not have to become
New Age victims!* In Chapter 14, I present an Action Plan
for parents. This Action Plan outlines positive steps you,
as a Christian parent, can take to put your child off-limits
to the New Age overlords.

Jesus loves you and me *and* He loves our children. He
loves you so much He willingly died on the cross that you
and your children might be saved. Who can separate you
and your loved ones from the love of Christ? Can the
deceivers of the New Age and the occultists who are so
readily found in our midst take us from the loving
protection of our God? No, not even the dark angels and
evil powers of Hell can do so (Romans 8:35, 37-39).

In Christ Jesus we are more than conquerors. We are children--regardless of our age--of the Most High. And as His children, we worship and praise Him who has placed us so carefully and with such loving kindness under His invincible wings of protection.

Texe Marrs
Austin, Texas

The Hellish Blueprint for the New Age Assault on Our Children

*But whoso shall offend one of these little ones which
believe in Me, it were better for him that a millstone
were hanged about his neck and that he were
drowned in the depth of the sea.*   (Matt. 18:6)

*When you put on your Skeletor helmet and
armoured belt you become transformed into an
agent of evil. Use your power sword and shield to
combat good. With your mystical ram's head scepter
you will be able to call forth the denizens of darkness
to help conquer the forces of good.*
    (Instructions for "Skeletor" toy
Masters of the Universe, Mattel Toys, Inc.)

Pity and have mercy on the children, and
pray for their protection, because Satan--
the Father of Lies and the grotesque
inventor of all wickedness--has targeted the innocents
for bondage, pain and destruction. Abundant evidence
exists that the startling hidden agenda of the Evil One
calls for total world domination by the year 2000. That's

only a decade away. Therefore, if he is to accomplish this hideous objective, Satan knows he must *today* win over the rising generation.

This is the reason for the shocking assault and all-out spiritual war being waged currently against our kids by Satan's demonic legions, his New Age leadership and their millions of disciples. This is also the reason why God has called me to write this book. *Satan's evil designs on our defenseless kids must be exposed and challenged by Christian believers everywhere.*

The Secret Plan

The New Age leadership has a meticulously detailed Secret Plan to ravage our kids and a magnificently orchestrated·network of Satanic workers to execute each and every detail of the Plan. Today, the seeds of this sinister Plan, planted almost four decades ago, are bearing cruel fruit. New Age occultism is sweeping across America and the globe, snatching up our innocent children in its rotten net. But now, with God's help, we can blow the lid off this dark Satanic conspiracy and set about rescuing our kids.

Satan's program of ongoing, systematic child abuse knows no bounds. We see all around us the evidence that Satan, under the guise of the New Age and the occult, has made the bondage of our children's souls a top priority. Images, concepts, and symbols of the New Age and of sorcery and the occult now permeate kids TV programs, cartoons, and movies. They are found in comic books, library books and toys, and in all kinds of music, especially rock music and so-called New Age "mood" music.

The school classroom is not immune from the pervasive influence of the killers of the spirit. Indeed, schools have tragically become battlefields of conflict and an astonishing and growing number have been transformed by New Age forces into evil inner sanctums where unsuspecting children are constantly being exploited and abused by willful teachers and school administrators bent on poisoning captive young minds with occultic, New Age doctrines and ritual.

Our precious kids are no longer safe even at the doctor's office. Each day new horror stories pour in of doctors, nurses, psychiatrists and other New Age holistic health care "professionals" abusing children. To these men and women trained in such New Age medical malpractices as guided imagery, visualization, meditation, crystal powers, reflexology, polarity therapy, biofeedback, spirit channeling, rebirthing, and past-life analysis, kids are like guinea pigs to be mentally and physically tortured and ritually abused.

Children are paying a tremendous price as a result of the New Age's grip on society. Many teens now suffer from oppression by demons, caused by involvement in Satanic worship and ritual and by the grotesque, black influence of heavy metal rock music. Meanwhile, the suicide rate among teens has exploded to unparalleled heights. Contemplating the future, one shudders to think what will be the fate of today's defenseless kids-- boys and girls of kindergarten and elementary school age--whose tender and susceptible minds are being subjected to ceaseless bombardment from the occult and the New Age.

Caught in a Satanic Vise

Discerning parents fully realize that families and especially children are today caught in the grip of a Satanic vise of frightening proportions. This is a demonic age. A momentous struggle of great historical and cosmic significance is occurring. This mighty struggle is between the holy and righteous forces of our Lord Jesus Christ and the diabolical and repugnant--but determined-- forces of Satanic powers. Bible prophecy told us such an awful day would come, when Satan is unleashed to do his worst:

> Therefore rejoice, ye heavens, and ye that dwell in them. Woe to the inhabitors of the earth and of the sea! for the devil is come down unto you, having great wrath, because he knoweth that he hath but a short time. (Rev. 12:12)

Our mission as Christians who love God and know that He loves our children is to understand the lateness of the hour. Recognizing that the night is upon us, we must take effective measures to protect and shield our loved ones as the storm clouds gather and as the unbridled rage of Satan passes overhead. The Wicked One and his Son of Perdition, the Antichrist, like unchained dragons, can be expected to lash out with all the evil forces at their command as they are driven back to the pit. Praise God, the Bible reveals that one day, after Satan has had his final, brief day of fury on planet earth, Jesus Christ, King of Kings, will deprive him of his kingdom here on earth and deliver to him a resounding defeat (Rev. 19:11-21).

The Hellish Blueprint of the Tibetan Master

The first and most important step we must take in protecting our kids is to understand that the present New Age assault on our children did not happen by accident. This has been schemed, planned and mapped out far, far in advance. Satan has from the beginning known that if he could capture an entire generation of kids, planet earth would soon be as a ripe plum, his for the taking.

Though 50 million lives were lost in the flames of World War II, Satan's disciple, Adolph Hitler, failed in his occult mission to usher in a New Age Kingdom under the guise of his Nazi Third Reich.[1] God's timetable simply would not allow Satan to conquer the saints of God at that time. However, the astonishing success of the New Age movement over the past few decades has mightily strengthened the possibility that *this generation of youth* may well be the one to fall completely under the iron grip of the devil.

The Bible tells us that children are very dear and precious to Jesus. Lovingly embracing little children who had come to Him, Christ told His disciples to care for little ones and to not forbid them to seek after Him, "for of such is the kingdom of heaven" (Matthew 19:14).

It must grieve our Heavenly Father deeply to see what is now happening to our children. For centuries Satan has labored, setting forth the foundation for this modern day assault. His goal has ever been the same: to wipe out all vestiges of Christ from the earth and thereby cause future generations to worship him, Lucifer, as God.

This rotten goal is at the very core of the elaborate program that the devil first launched in the Garden of Eden, expanded on in ancient Babylon, and is working at non-stop today. Over forty years ago Satan began his latest and most damaging assault, directing one of his chief demon-aides, Djwahl Khul, called "The Tibetan," to make contact with those humans in the New Age movement who serve his hellish master.

A Demon Master Speaks: The Roots of Evil Spread

The year 1945 saw the closing chapters of the second World War and the finish of the Nazi menace. However, it was also in this year that a second menace, secretive and more guarded but just as frightening and diabolical, took root and began quickly to spread its poisonous tentacles in all directions. This new plague of Satan was brought to humanity by a demon entity who, taking on the name of Djwahl Khul, the Tibetan Master, appeared to Alice Bailey, head of the New Age's Lucis Trust (formerly Lucifer Publishing Company) and through her dictated a number of books and messages.[2]

In the years since, the books written under the command of this demon have multiplied so that today, New Age and occult bookstores offer a large selection of these publications. Among their revealing titles: *Initiation, Human and Solar; Letters on Occult Meditation; Discipleship in the New Age; A Treatise on White Magic;* and *The Destiny of Nations.* What's more, many influential New Age leaders got hold of these books and were led by their own possessing demons to author still more books and writings.

Alice Bailey passed away in 1978, but her demonic Master Djwahl Khul evidently continues his vile labors on behalf of his overlord, Lucifer, the devil. One only need buy and read current New Age magazines or attend New Age seminars and church services held in every American city, large or small, to discover that the Tibetan Master is alive and well in the hearts of New Age teachers. The Tibetan's teachings are widespread and pervasive.

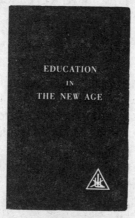

This Lucis Trust book contains a summary of the New Age Plan to destroy our kids.

Djwahl Khul's most significant and most spiritually damaging contribution to the New Age Plan to rob our children of their salvation is contained in the Alice Bailey book, *Education in the New Age.*[3] There we find a carefully laid out road map to destruction for our kids. If we wish to truly understand what the New Age has planned for our kids and how those plans are being executed today, this is the starting point.

Close examination of this New Age blueprint reveals 13 bold pillars upon which Satan intends to build a new humanity, with our children as his sacrificial lambs. Here is what Satan, through his demon, the Tibetan Master, prescribed for mankind's future and what he says the New Age has in store for our children:

1) *The children of the future will serve a One World (Planetary) Government and live in a One World culture.*

We need . . . the political synthesis of a World Federation with the . . . World Brain. . . . We need also a planetary way of life, a planetary ethics and a planetary way of feeling to supply the powerful drive we shall require for the great tasks that lie ahead of us.[4]

2) *Patriotism to one's country must be abolished and all national barriers destroyed in order to build a New One World Order.*

When the young people are civilized, cultured, and responsive to *World Citizenship*, we shall have a world of men awakened, creative and possessing a true sense of values. . . .We are today on our way to a far better civilization than the world has ever known and toward conditions which will insure a much happier humanity and which will see the end of national differences. . . .[5]

World Citizenship . . . should be the goal of the enlightened everywhere and the hallmark of the spiritual man.[6]

3) *Children will accept that Eastern mystical religion is to be married to the Christianity of the West to forge a new, unified social and religious order of "Universal Truths."*

In this education for the New Age the . . . East-West philosophy by the Tibetan will find its pagan setting . . . the two great civilizations of yesterday (are) ready to give birth to the *one* civilization of tomorrow.[7]

4) *Teenagers and youth will rebel and revolt against their parents and against authority to help usher in the New Age World Order:*

Today it is beginning to be possible to lay the foundation for this new teaching, because the young people in every land are forcing upon their parents and their teachers the idea of their essential and determined independence. The revolt of youth . . . in spite of all the immediate and individual disasters, has been a desirable thing and has prepared the way.[8]

5) *Youth and all of humanity must accept that the time will inevitably come when grown-ups who refuse to become part of the New Age will have to be killed. They are to be considered as lowly germs, an infection or blot on humanity that must be stamped out and eradicated:*

A violent streptococcic germ and infection . . . makes its presence felt in infected areas in the body of humanity. Another surgical operation may be necessary . . . to dissipate the infection and get rid of the fever. . . . Let us never forget . . . that when a (life) form proves inadequate, or too diseased, or too crippled . . . it is--from the point of view of the hierarchy--no disaster when that form has to go.[9]

Death is not a disaster to be feared; the Work of the destroyer is not really cruel or undesirable. . . .

Therefore, there is much destruction permitted by the Custodians of the Plan and much evil turned into good.[10]

6) *The traditional family unit is not desirable for the Aquarian, or New Age. Children belong to the government, to the world and the community--the human group--not to their parents. A new kind of family unit must inevitably come into existence.*

In the coming world state, the individual . . . will subordinate his personality to the good of the whole.[11]

The first group . . . of which any individual child becomes normally aware is the family group as a unit in the community. . . . The family group has shared in the general separativeness, selfishness, and individual isolated exclusiveness. . . .[12]

Family pride (is) overemphasized, leading to the different barriers which today separate man from man, family from group. . . . However, under the coming world order educators will prepare the young people . . . for participation in . . . a harmonious world.[13]

7) *Young people must be taught to believe in reincarnation and karma (the Law of Rebirth) rather than the resurrection and judgment teachings of the Bible. This belief must guide behavior, especially the sexual conduct.*

One of the tasks of the educator of the future will be to teach the meaning of the Law of Rebirth (reincarnation and karma), and thus bring about . . . a profound change in the racial attitude to life and sex, to birth and parenthood.[14]

The doctrine of reincarnation . . . will be one of the keynotes of the New World Religion.[15]

8) *Absurd and immature notions of "sin" and "guilt" must not be imparted to children by parents, teachers, pastors and other adults. A more permissive and worldly attitude must be adopted.*

It is the older generation who foster in a child an early and most unnecessary sense of guilt, of sinfulness, and wrong doing. . . . The many small and petty sins, imposed upon children by the constant reiteration of "NO," by the use of the word "naughty," and based largely on parental failure . . . are of no real moment.[16]

9) *Children are to be taught that all religions-- Christianity, Witchcraft, Hinduism, Buddhism, Islam, Judaism, Paganism, etc.--are equally worthwhile and that it doesn't matter in which god one believes.*

The children of the different nations will be taught truth, without bias or prejudice. . . . World Unity will be a fact when the children of the world are taught that religious differences are largely a matter of birth. Gradually, our quarrels and differences will be offset and the idea of the One Humanity will take their place.[17]

The (New Age) Christ has no religious barriers in His consciousness. It matters not what faith a man may call himself.[18]

10) *The new generation of youth must recognize that Jesus did not come to save or convert anyone; because no one is lost.*

He did not come to convert the heathen world for, in the eyes of the Christ and of His true disciples, no such world exists.[19]

11) *Christian doctrines, such as that of heaven, hell, and judgment, must be discarded and the theology of the Old Testament must be repudiated.*

Christianity . . . has made eternal happiness dependent upon the acceptance of a theological dogma: Be a true professing Christian and live in a somewhat fatuous heaven or refuse to be an accepting Christian and go to an impossible hell--a hell growing out of the theology of the Old Testament and its presentation of a God, full of hate and jealousy. Both concepts are today repudiated by all sane, sincere, thinking people.[20]

No one of any true reasoning power or with any true belief in a God of love accepts the heaven of the churchmen or has any desire to go there. Still less do they accept the "lake that burneth with fire and brimstone."[21]

12) *A New Age World Religion must be established without Jesus Christ as Lord and Savior. The Christian Church is dead and must be replaced.*

The Church today is the tomb of Christ. Humanity is in desperate need and the need must be met. The theologies now taught . . . are crystalized and of relatively little use. Priests and church men, orthodox instructors and fundamentalists (fanatical though sincere) are seeking to perpetuate that which is old and which sufficed in the past . . . but which now fails to do so.[22]

We are also visioning a new and vital world religion, a universal faith which will have its roots in the past, but which will make clear the new dawning beauty and the coming vital revelation.[23]

13) *The coming New Age World Religion will emphasize the unity of all religions while rejecting Jesus Christ's profound Biblical statement, "I am the way, the truth and the life."*

The great theme of the new world religion will be the recognition of the many divine approaches. . . . The platform of the new world religion will be built by many groups, working under the inspiration of the (New Age) Christ.[24]

* * * *

It is apparent from these thirteen foul doctrines that Satan's demon chieftain, Djwahl Khul, and his many New Age followers despise Jesus Christ. This leads them to seek to destroy our children by undermining Christian principles in all spheres of society. They plot to decompose and destroy the family unit, subvert Bible doctrine, and promote a One World New Age Religion and Government.

Children are expected to rebel against their parents, do as they please without fear or guilt, and freely worship false gods without condemnation. As we will discover later, our children are also taught by New Age leaders to picture themselves as gods, a blasphemous lie that leads to selfishness and to destruction.

New Age . . . or Old Age?

But, are these lies of Satan really "new?" Or, has Satan merely resurrected the same deceitful lies that he has always used to enslave the souls of young people? The fact is, the New Age is nothing more than the *Old Age* dressed up in flimsy new garb.

We can easily trace the roots of New Age occultism all the way back to ancient Babylon, the headquarters from where Satan first set up his worldwide church. Nimrod, the first of the great Babylonian rulers, was also declared to be the first of the man-gods. The teaching was given out that Nimrod had attained his crown and his authority because he was an advanced evolutionary being, superior to other men. His sultry but vicious wife, Semiramis, was the first of the Great Mother Goddesses.[25]

After Nimrod died, Semiramis bore a son out of wedlock with one of her many lovers and also named the son Nimrod, announcing to the world that this son was the reincarnated spirit of the deceased ruler. However, the people were nevertheless required to worship and pay homage to the departed Nimrod and to other exalted man-gods residing in the spirit world.

We see in these events the roots of several cardinal New Age doctrines: evolution, human divinity, spirit worship, reincarnation and sexual license. Also, we find the origin of another key New Age belief: the belief in an unholy Trinity, or Godhead, of three divinities: Father, Mother, Son.

In ancient Babylon and Egypt where the Mother Goddess religion flourished, the symbol of the triangle denoted this unholy trinity which mocked the true biblical Godhead of God, His Son Jesus Christ and the Holy Spirit. It is not surprising that the triangle has throughout the ages been used by Satan worshipers as a holy symbol to be revered. Today, we often see this symbol prominently displayed on satanic rock albums and in New Age books, magazines and jewelry.

Mystery Babylon Lives Through Our Kids!

What does all this mean for us today? Plenty! Just as we see the triangle in common use, such ungodly doctrines as reincarnation and sexual abandon are finding popular expression. We also are not surprised to discover that many other doctrines, rituals, practices and symbols have been revived from the past by the New Age movement.

Our kids are being bombarded with these influences. Here is just a partial list of ancient satanic teachings, practices and symbols now in vogue and being pushed on our children and teens:

color therapy
heavy metal music
unisex dress
sadism
sorcery
incest and immorality
hypnotism
New Age "mood" music
palmistry
rebellion
astral travel
mystery teachings
ESP (psychic powers)
God as "Mother"
astrology
nature worship
rhythmic breathing
visualization
psychedelic drugs
sodomy
feminism
necromancy
dragons
pyramids
chanting
yoga
demonic music
fortune telling
levitation
self-love
fire walking
body tattoos
numerology
pedophilia
mental imagery

the unicorn, pegasus and other "magical" beasts
communication with the dead
meditation (other than on God's word)
satanic symbols (pentagram, triangle & circle, etc.)

The Astonishing Growth of the New Age Plan

The New Age practices, rituals and symbols listed above are only a few of the many methods and avenues by which Satan is luring our youth. This book will present authoritative, thoroughly documented proof that the monstrous New Age octopus has spread its tentacles in every direction. We find hideous and cancerous outgrowths in games, cartoons, movies, toys, books, music, and sports. Bubble gum cards now carry New Age propaganda messages, some Sunday School curricula has been changed to accomodate New Age doctrines, day care centers have become founts of New Age teachings, hospitals the purveyors of New Age ritual.

As we shall see in the next chapter, even such venerable institutions as the Boy Scouts, the Girl Scouts, the
YWCA, NASA's space agency, Walt Disney, and Sears
department stores have been invaded by the New Age
mind controllers. From womb and cradle to adolescence,
our children are being smothered by Satan's New Age
demonic forces. All this has been planned. Whether we
like the word or not, there *is* a gigantic *conspiracy*
underway.

The New Age Conspiracy Against Our Kids

The Bible prophesied that in the last days a massive
Satanic conspiracy would grow and gather steam until it
grew into a hideous monster of world-wide proportions.
Only Christian believers will be exempt from being drawn
into this incredible conspiracy. All others will believe the
Lie (see II Thes. 2).

Criminal law experts say that a conspiracy is defined
as two or more people colluding, or plotting together, to
carry out an unlawful act. *Two people.* But the end-time
New Age conspiracy already involves tens of millions of
anti-God lawbreakers. By the time Jesus returns, billions
will join the Jesus-hating forces of the New Age Beast:

> And all that dwell on the earth shall worship him, whose
> names are not written in the book of life of the Lamb
> slain from the foundation of the world. (Rev. 13:8)

A conspiracy always has leaders. The New Age
religion of Satan is no exception. It has its shadowy leadership in the demonic spirit world, consisting of Satan,
the lord of this world, and his many demons. Then, on
earth, there are hundreds of top-ranked New Age leaders, managers, and teachers in all realms of society who
take instruction from their demonic spirit guides.

Marilyn Ferguson, author of the bestselling New Age "bible," *The Aquarian Conspiracy,* says that the transformation of society into a New Age kingdom will only come about when the fourth and final level of organization is achieved--the level of *conspiracy.* This level is attained, she explains, when all the various disciples of the New Age begin to come together. "In the fourth stage, conspiracy," Ferguson writes, New Age disciples begin to reason, "why can't minds *join* to heal and transform society?"[26]

Michael Murphey, co-founder of the New Age research community, Esalen, believes that conspiracy will inevitably lead to "renewal" of self and community. "Let's make that conspiracy apparent," he encourages his followers, "we can turn our daily common life into the dance the world is meant for."[27]

What Murphey fails to explain of course, is that the only dance steps New Agers know are the ones that permit them to dance with the devil, their unworldly Fred Astaire-Ginger Rogers substitute dancing instructor. Since the devil cannot be in all places at all times, however, he makes available his assistants--the *Masters.* They, like their overlord, are nimble, agile Satanic dance instructors.

The Powerful and Influential New Age Network

It is important we understand that, although Alice Bailey's demon guide, Djwhal Khul, transmitted to her and the Lucis Trust organization what is possibly the most clear elaboration of Satan's New Age Plan for our kids, Satan's dark angels also work through many other groups and individuals. As Alice Bailey herself admitted:

> We are only one of many groups through which the
> Masters of Wisdom are working. . . . Other disciples and

groups have been responsible for initiating other projects under the guidance of their own masters.[28]

The many New Age groups and organizations are *networking*, that is, conspiring together, always with the Plan in mind. "Absorbing devotion to the Plan" is mandatory.[29] Therefore, we should be careful not to waste our time concentrating and fixing our eyes on the human leadership pushing the Plan. After all, they are mere cogs in Satan's great machine. He alone is the mastermind of this vast universal conspiracy. Yet, it is instructive to know how many powerful and wealthy potentates, celebrities, and other influential personalities are active in the New Age. They are signs of Satan's mighty stranglehold on this planet.

The ranks of the New Age include such notables as: Prince Phillip of Great Britain; Ted Turner, head of Cable News Network (CNN) and now top-dog in an atrocity called the Better World Society; Willy Brandt, former Chancellor of West Germany and now with the World Federalists; John Fetzer, communications baron, former owner of the Detroit Tigers baseball team, and now founder of a New Age foundation endowed with over $150 million; Robert Muller, former Assistant Secretary-General of the United Nations; U. S. Senator Claiborne Pell, a dabbler in psychic phenomena and the occult and a strong supporter of New Age projects on Capital Hill; Dr. Jonas Salk, inventor of the polio vaccine; Edgar Mitchell, former NASA astronaut; Norman Vincent Peale, positive thinking pioneer who advocates communication with the dead; George Lucas, movie director of *Star Wars* and *Willow*; and Laurence Rockefeller, multimillionaire, who gave New Age Catholic Priest Matthew Fox a grant so he could write the Satanic book, *The Coming of the Cosmic Christ*.

The Rich, the Famous, the Powerful

Do these people sound to you like bizarre, flakey Shirley MacLaine wackos? No, it's undeniable that the New Age has attracted many of the most creative, powerful, highly motivated men and women in the world.

We didn't even mention the Hollywood New Age types of which there are far too many to list. But here's a sampling: Tina Turner, Cher, Phylicia Rashad, Sharon Gless, Ally Sheedy, Willie Nelson, Richard Gere, John Denver, Gilda Radner, Michael Jackson, Sigourney Weaver, Linda Evans . . . the names go on indefinitely. It is unfortunate that these men and women are often presented as role models for our kids.

Then there are the professional athletes and sports stars, the rock music entertainers, the writers and playwrights, the psychologists and lawyers and so on. Surely, Satan has today put together an immense juggernaut of destructive evil unparalleled in all the annals of human history.

The sad and tragic thing is that some of these people do not even realize they are part of the great conspiracy to bring in the New Age Kingdom of Satan. They have been brainwashed to believe they are promoting world and inner peace, and love. A few do not even know what the term "New Age" means.

They are like the German townspeople who each day, unknowingly and in ignorant bliss, strolled near the gates of the Nazi concentration camps on their way to work at munitions factories. These people did not understand and so they continued to willingly--even eagerly--heap honor, praise, authority and a throne upon the head to one of the most ruthless, occultic men of all time: Adolph Hitler. They, like today's New Age disciples, were fed the Big Lie. And they swallowed it whole.

The Hidden Agenda of Their Master: An Occultly Guarded Secret

So many are today deluded and deceived by the New Age because they fail to realize that Satan's Plan is not always easily discerned. Regrettably, most of our Christian leaders do not even understand the most basic rudiments of what the New Age is all about. It has taken me three years of dedicated, full-time research to discover where all the tentacles of the beast lead, and who is in charge of each tentacle. Moreover, Satan is clever enough to create fresh new tentacles when one or more are exposed to the Light of Truth and wither.

The New Age demon Masters do not even let many of their highest ranking human counterparts in on all aspects of how the Plan is being executed. Djwhal Khul explains that the activities of the human custodians of the Plan are *occultly* guarded.[30] (The word occult simply means hidden or concealed, kept from view.) "Think not that I can tell you of the Plan as it truly is," says Khul, it is a "hidden secret."[31]

New Age theologian David Spangler reveals that "gradually, silently . . . behind the scenes," the Plan has been worked by human disciples and their spirit masters:

> It has been a secret project, deeply hidden and
> unheralded, lest these sacred energies be diverted or
> tapped wrongly or ahead of schedule.[32]

Exposing the Plan: "For There is Nothing Covered that Shall not be Revealed"

Thanks to our Lord Jesus Christ, the boast of Spangler and the demon Djwhal Khul that the New Age Plan is to be kept a secret and occultly guarded, is proving to be an idle one. God wants His people to know the Truth; the Bible tells us we arc not ignorant of the devil's devices.

I am so appreciative to God our Father that He has given me insight into the Master Plan of Evil to destroy our children. He has opened the doors to my understanding so I could go on to reveal these hidden things to you in this book. Just as Jesus Christ our Lord promised:

> For there is nothing covered that shall not be revealed; neither hid, that shall not be known. Therefore, whatsoever ye have spoken in darkness shall be heard in the light; and that which ye have spoken in the ear in closets shall be proclaimed upon the housetops.
>
> (Luke 12:2, 3)

The Bible instructs us to have no part with the New Age. There is no common ground, no room for compromise, no "dialogue" to be spoken. Instead, if we wish to protect our children, we are called to "contend for the faith" (Jude 1:3) and are warned--because Jesus loves us--to "have no fellowship with the unfruitful works of darkness, but rather reprove them" (Eph. 5:11).

The Battle for the Next Generation

Parents are today caught up in spiritual warfare with the cruelest and most deceitful military strategist who has ever lived: Satan. The stakes are high for the winner and an entire generation of innocent children is on the line. The only way we can win this Battle of the Ages is to depend on resources from Almighty God above. Those resources are more than sufficient. Indeed, Jesus came as God in the flesh to earth expressly to destroy the works of the devil and He is our strength and our refuge today as He reigns in heaven.

Meanwhile, to effectively accomplish the work of the Lord here on earth below, we must be knowledgeable of Satan's ages-old but still operative battle plan. We must also recognize his designs for the future. As I've discussed in this chapter, we must keep in mind that:

● The New Age is not new at all, but is simply a revival of Satan's ages-old occultic church which took root and once reigned notoriously supreme in ancient Babylon.

● The current explosion of New Age occultism and today's brain robbery of our kids actually had its origins over four decades ago as Satan's New Age disciples began to execute a carefully orchestrated and designed, hellish blueprint to pollute and destroy our children.

● This blueprint for destruction continues to be worked out today as New Age leaders fan out into all areas of children's existence, insidiously preparing youth to faithfully serve Satan in the coming New Age Kingdom on earth.

T W O

From the Womb and Cradle to the Grave

Lo, children are an heritage of the Lord and the fruit of the womb is His reward.   (Psalm 127:3)

The first thing to do after discovering you are pregnant is to give thanks to the Goddess . . . Rainbow Mother, nurturing mother, mother of us all, suckle your rebel-lions. . . . Let your milk and honey flow through this Promised land.
                    (Joshua Halpern, *Children of the Dawn*)

It is the aim of the New Age leadership to totally immerse our kids into the boiling cauldron of New Age lies and poisons from the moment they are conceived until the day they die. From the selection of the baby's name to Sunday School lessons for kids and clothing and jewelry for teens, we now find disturbing New Age influences hostile to the eternal Truths of God's Word. The corrupt-minded men and women who mastermind the New Age do not want to give our kids even a fleeting chance to come to know the real God of this universe, Jesus Christ. This is why, from the womb and cradle to the grave children are surrounded--their senses are bombarded--by pulsating demonic images and teachings.

The savage bombardment begins before the child

enters the world an infant. For example, many New Age parenting books recommend that pregnant mothers continually play New Age music to the fetus 24 hours a day, even during sleep. They also encourage the parents to dedicate the baby to "the Goddess" or to the "New Age Kingdom" while yet in the womb.

In his highly acclaimed *Children of the Dawn: Visions of the New Family*, New Age childcare and parenting expert Joshua Halpern prescribes a number of new parenting techniques and practices.[1] For example, he calls for a nature blessing event to be conducted by parents and friends to celebrate the new baby, which he explains is not new at all. Birth, Halpern teaches, is simply the "return to new life" of a reincarnated person. In his book, one of Halpern's clients describes one such nature blessing event that was held:

> The day came. . . . We gathered our symbols of holiness and walked down to the barn. Grandpa . . . smudged each person in the circle with sage and cedar. This is a North American Indian custom for cleaning energy in a sacred manner . . . The silence was answered with the chant 'ya-na-ha-we-ah-heyenae." It means Great Spirit.
>
> During the chant, Chuck and I made our altar. . . .On it we placed the directional feathers, pointing in the four directions plus two more for the Earth Mother. . . . I then began prayers (to) the spirits.[2]

The horrible, inevitable truth is that New Age parents everywhere today are dedicating their "divine" babies to Satan. Few understand the gravity--the utter horror--of what they are doing. Through a variety of rituals and incantations, they call on one or more of an array of spirit entities as well as the Goddess or the Mother, dedicating their child to the service of the spirits or the "Mother." Like the perverse Canaanites in the Old Testament, they are spiritually--sometimes physically--sacrificing their children to the devil. Yet they are convinced that what they do is holy and sacred. Thus, Joshua Halpern writes:

> The first thing to do after discovering you are pregnant is to give thanks to the Goddess. . . . Soon, very soon, there will be millions and millions of us who are ready to acknowledge our common roots in the Soul of Love. The day is fast approaching when all of humanity will realize they originate within the Rainbow Mother. By celebrating the return of new life and the ways of the Goddess we help usher in the Light of Truth. By praising the Holiness of the womb we establish ourselves upon the fundamental ground of being.[3]

> Rainbow Mother, nurturing mother, mother of us all, suckle your rebel-lions. . . . Let your milk and honey flow through this Promised land.[4]

Halpern also offers to his readers ceremonies and occult New Age rituals once the baby is born. For example, he believes that the circumcision should be performed as a holy New Age act. Here's what he advises regarding the circumcision of boys:

> Circumcision is a mystical ceremony and must be performed by a Holy Man/Woman. The one who makes the incision must keep God's Name resonating constantly. They must consciously meditate upon the Third Eye. . . . The genitals are directly connected to the Third Eye-Brain Center. . . .
> When the rite is practiced with God Consciousness the baby boy is initiated into (sexual) tantra. He learns somatically that the Light in his mind and the power of his loins are One. If the rite is practiced with Holy intention the boy child will emerge from the ceremony keyed into God. He will experience no trauma. Indeed he will feel a sublime joy.[5]

Reincarnation: An Excuse to Kill Unborn Babies

The Satanic spirit that inspires the New Age is the very same spirit that also inspires the killing of unborn babies. The popular name for this is "abortion" of a "fetus." The bible clearly teaches that at the moment of conception life begins, but the New Age view is radically different.

The New Age doctrine of reincarnation provides the perfect excuse for abortion. The law of Karma states that each person *chooses* their fate in the life to come. For example, to balance the evil act, a murderer in one lifetime may, upon death, choose to become murdered in the next life cycle. Since the baby in the womb is now known to have a heartbeat and thus be "alive" at three weeks, according to this New Age law, the killing of the baby is merely the carrying out of the baby's *own desire*, before incarnation. In other words, the theory is that *the baby chose to be aborted!*

Easy death is the New Age law of life. What does it hurt to kill the unborn while they are still in the womb? The person's spirit, the New Age contends, will simply be reborn later into another body. Indeed, this same grisly justification can be used by New Age occultists for the Satanic sacrifice of infants.

New Age Names for the Baby

Have you noticed today's proliferation of strange-sounding names for babies? Ever wonder where many of these unusual names come from? Not content to bequeath to their children names emanating from Judeo-Christian culture, today's New Age parents are increasingly seeking newer names based on the ancient pagan cultures.

One of the top selling books on the market today is *The New Age Baby Name Book* by Sue Browder which contains over 3,000 baby names.[6] Published by Warner

Books, one of America's largest secular publishers, this unholy guide has been used by hundreds of thousands of parents to choose a New Age name for their baby. It is a sad, almost unimaginable and revolting thing to saddle an innocent baby with the demonic name of a Hindu, Egyptian, Norse, or other pagan god or goddess or with an astrological, occult or other "magical" name. Satan's New Age will stop at nothing to destroy our kids. However, naming babies to honor and reverence the great destroyer himself is the height of reprobate cruelty.

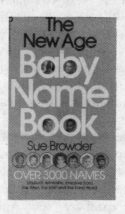

THE NEW AGE BABY NAME BOOK.

Sue Browder's shocking New Age baby name book is designed to ably serve the Lord of the Underworld. In recommending an occult or other magical name, she suggests:

> If you are looking for a magical or astrological name, you will find . . . some delightful magic names used in incantations to summon or exorcise spirits, plus deity names from the Egyptian Book of the Dead. . . . Hindu names also offer dozens of possibilities, since the Hindus often name their children after gods to bring them luck and salvation.[7]

Common (Hindu) boys names include Kistna, Hanuman, Siva, Rama, Narain and Valli, while Devi, Sakti, and Ratri are popular for girls.[8]

Browder also recommends for the New Age baby such Hindu names as Ram (meaning "God"), Singh ("lion"), Gupta ("Protector"), Ananda ("bliss"), and Das ("slave").[9]

A growing number of New Age adults are now changing their names as well. One woman now calls herself Shakti Gawain, "Shakti" meaning "one with the goddess." Shakti Gawain is author of the New Age book, *Creative Visualization*, which has sold over 800,000 copies. Another New Age believer with a new name is Maitreya Stillwater. Stillwater is a popular New Age musician who named himself after "Lord Maitreya," the spirit masquerading as the New Age "Christ." Other New Age adults have taken on such planetary names as "Moon", "Sun", and "Star" while still others borrow names derived from the Hindu guru whom they worship.

New Age Sunday School

The Plan is that once the baby is dedicated to heathen gods and given a New Age name, he or she is then gradually but surely indoctrinated in the New Age religious philosophies. One way this is done--believe it or not--is through Sunday School curriculum.

The infiltration by the New Age community into our churches by subverting and sabotaging our Sunday School materials for kids evidently has a high priority. One New Age organization in Virginia, the Association for Research and Enlightenment (*A.R.E.*), set up to propagate the teachings of the late psychic/seer Edgar Cayce, publishes religious educational books and materials now used by some Christian churches. Cleverly and artfully concealed as Sunday School texts, the materials are packed with scripture references.

In one *A.R.E.* book for young adults, the authors, Shirley Clement and Virginia Field, propose to educate the youth on the "spiritual laws of life."[10] Entitled *Beginning the Search*, this horrendous book has a chart instructing kids on the "positive" meanings of occult symbols. It includes charts, games, puzzles and other activities to spur and retain the interest of young readers. Such exercises sugar-coat and make attractive the unholy New Age teachings presented elsewhere in the book, such as the following:

Kundalini, or Serpent Power:

> Let's examine a way that our thoughts can affect our bodies. Within the . . . center is the energy force known as *Kundalini* or "serpent fire"--a strong, creative energy. . . . When we meditate we can arouse the Kundalini.[11]

Our Thoughts Create Reality (Man is a Co-Creator with God):

> Our thoughts have the power to create. Our every thought is a blessing or a curse to ourselves and others. Whatever we image or concentrate on, good or bad, positive or negative, we will eventually experience.[12]

Chanting and Other Meditation Rituals:

> Meditation Aids--you may try to use some of these pre-meditation activities: (1) Chant, using these syllables: "Ar-r-r--Ou-u-Ur-r," "Ar-r-r-r-r-r-Ar," or "Aa-ree-ooh-mm." (2) Listen to beautiful, soothing music (3) Burn incense or a scented candle.[13]

There is no Antichrist, Satan, or Devil:

The only anti-Christ (anti-love), "Satan" or "devil" we
ever have to face is our own selfishness. . . . Christ is all
and in all. When we realize this, we can change our lives.
We can start living in harmony with the laws of the
Oneness. . . . [14]

*Reincarnation is required to undo problems created in past
lives and thus balance one's karma:*

Selfish thoughts and desires triggered negative karma,
creating problems. . . . The law of karma requires that
created problems be met until they are overcome.[15]

*The "Christ-Soul" Jesus is really the spirit "Amilius" who
was reincarnated and became "expressed as" the Master
Jesus:*

Amilius, who later expressed as Jesus, was the
individualized spiritual expression of God through
which all earthly creations came into being. . . . He chose
to express in a physical body. . . . He became known
(first) as Adam. . . . Step by step the Christ-soul (first
called Amilius, then Adam) would re-enter materiality
to help awaken mankind.[16]

We are all "God," the Universe is "God," "God" is a force:

There is only one force, one mind, one presence--God.
All that is in the cosmos is of God and is one with him.[17]

The Infiltration and Sabotage of Sunday School Curricula

Even the traditionally "safe" Sunday School curricula
published by standard Christian publishing houses can
no longer be considered safe and left unexamined.

Recently, a young married couple who teach a third grade Sunday School class at a fundamentalist Baptist Church came to me with the Sunday School Quarterly which the children in their class are asked to read. They were alarmed over its content. Rightfully so. I was appalled at the occultic symbols and also at the numerous references to visualization and mental imagery.

In one section, kids were told to imagine they were walking in the forest when, suddenly, they stepped on a huge and dangerous poisonous snake. The child's startled feeling at being surprised by the snake, the book suggested, is how the Holy Spirit works in their lives!

The Sunday School teachers who brought this passage to my attention simply could not believe that any Christian writer would insinuate in a Sunday School lesson for kids that the Holy Spirit can in any way, form or fashion, be equated with the feeling one experiences when being surprised and startled by a poisonous snake. The "god" of the Satanists may well be pictured as a snake, but *the* Holy Spirit of God?

In fact, the god of the New Age *is* symbolized by the snake. In India, a number of Hindus worship the deadly poisonous cobra snake. It is a symbol of their god. Meanwhile, in America and throughout the world, the New Age teaches its disciples that it is *kundalini*, or *serpent power*, that results in rebirth or transformation of the individual. To be "born again"--initiated--into the New Age is to yield to this serpent power.

What is more shocking is the fact that the publisher of this Sunday School material has over the years gained a reputation for its solid, theologically accurate Sunday School publications. How could the trained editors and the reviewers, let alone the writers, have allowed such degradations?

Regrettably, I did not have the time to conduct in-depth research on all the Sunday School curriculum of this particular publisher. I did report to them the atrocious examples cited above and asked them to remove these sections. However, this is not the only producer of Sunday School curriculum to plant or include New Age and occult doctrines and teachings in their materials. Every adult who teaches Sunday school should realize the grave responsibility that is theirs and examine all Sunday School literature before distributing it to the kids in their class. No longer can we trust the integrity and reliability of the publishers. Each of us must be a watchman on the wall.

A Revised Lord's Prayer for the New Age

As if their tampering with and sabotaging Sunday School curricula isn't bad enough, New Agers also are seeking to distort the Lord's Prayer, given by Jesus to His disciples when they asked Him to teach them to pray (Matthew 6:9-13). Reda Lucy's New Age book called *The Lord's Prayer for Children* is an example of this assault on a prayer of our Lord's that Christians universally accept as precious and sacred.[18]

In her children's guide to the Lord's Prayer, Reda Lucy takes each phrase and line of the prayer and interprets its meaning in light of the New Age religion. The result is a severe distortion of scripture.

Commenting on the prayer phrase *Our Father which art in heaven,* Lucy denies the existence of a personal God and a real heaven, and explains to children that *they, too, are "God."*

> Heaven is the home of God and heaven is our home, too. Heaven is also an action of your happiness . . . like petting your dog, riding your tricycle or bike, and playing games. . . . God is many things to many people. . . . God is everything, everywhere. This means you, too, are God . . . Your thought and your speaking is a form of energy, and this, too, is God.[19]

Incredibly, Lucy suggests that the word "thy" in the phrase *Hallowed be Thy name* be interpreted as the *name of the child.* Then she invites the child to write his or her name--Holly, Leroy, Denise, or whatever--in a blank space provided in the book. She explains that this will indicate the child's acceptance of the principle that it is *the child's name* that is respected, loved, and is good (e.g., "Hallowed"), not the name of a personal external God.[20]

The Lord's Prayer According to Edgar Cayce and A.R.E.

The A.R.E. also is doing its best to rework, revise and subvert the true meaning of the Lord's Prayer. Its religious teaching guide for the young states:

> The Lord's Prayer is recommended in the Cayce readings as an ideal prayer affirmation to use before meditation. When we pray "Our Father," we recognize the brotherhood of all mankind, the presence of God in everyone. . . .
> "Forgive us . . . as we forgive our debtors" shows that we recognize the laws of karma. . . .
> "For thine is the kingdom, and the power, and the glory" reminds us that God is the spiritual essence within us. . . .[21]

According to the A.R.E.'s interpretation of the Lord's Prayer, each of the seven portions of the Lord's Prayer relates to the body's energy points or spiritual centers (called *Chakras* by other New Age teachers). When you recite the Lord's Prayer, you activate these energy points and connect with "God," the Force or universal mind.[22]

The Lord's Prayer According to Catholic Priest Matthew Fox and Friends

Other New Age teachers offer up similarly warped interpretations of the Lord's Prayer. In Catholic Priest Matthew Fox's heretical magazine, *Creation*, lingual specialist Neil Douglas-Klotz falsely asserts that when Jesus told His disciples to pray "in my name," He actually meant to pray "with my light, or method."[23] In other words, Douglas-Klotz denies that we are to use the power of Jesus' name in prayer.

He also offers us a uniquely New Age translation of the "Our Father" in the Lord's Prayer. This, Douglas-Klotz explains, does not necessarily mean the literal male word of "Father." Instead, he claims that in the Aramaic language, this word is comparable to the sacred Hindu phrase, or mantra, of A-U-M (OM), simply meaning a sound or vibration.[24] Of course, this erroneous reinterpretation of the truth fits in nicely with the New Age view that God is simply an energy force or vibration pattern. As for "Thy Kingdom Come," Douglas-Klotz believes this refers not to the second coming of Jesus to set up His Kingdom, but to our own ascension to "divine royalty"-- which he terms "the kingdom/queendom within."[25]

From Boy Scouts to Bubble Gum: The New Age Assault on Our Kids

If Sunday School materials and the Lord's Prayer are not sacrosanct to the New Age crowd that has taken aim at our kids, don't expect that anything else is either. Wherever we turn, whether to such American institutions as the Boy Scouts and Girl Scouts and YWCA, or to bubble gum cards, offices of pediatricians, the pages of the *Sears Catalog*, or examine the new jewelry for teens and apparel for kids, the New Age has boldly and arrogantly left its calling cards. Below are just a few examples of this horrendous and continuous invasion of the New Age soul snatchers.

Bazooka Joe Comics

A mini-*Bazooka Joe* comics inside a bubble gum package depicts two kids asking a third child why he's sitting in a lotus-type position.

"Practicing Meditation," the third child replies, "It fills me with inner peace. After two minutes my mind is completely blank."

"Gee, I thought he was born that way," said one of the two on-lookers.

Mother's Cookies

"Mother's Cookies" recently included for kids a baseball-type *Movie Tales* card inside each package of their cookies which promoted New Age spirit guides. The card mentioned that inside each person was a hidden entity, or "Prince." The card included this message: "There is an inner-self (Prince) inside each of us yearning to be discovered, known and unconditionally loved."

Topps Chewing Gum Cards

Collectible bubble gum cards put out by the Topps Chewing Gum Corporation feature the Garbage Pail Kids, gross examples of depravity for children. One mother who recently wrote me about these "humorous" cards for kids remarked, "I was surprised and shocked at the open and blatant suggestions about suicide and the occult and the horrifying violence, all presented in a 'funny' context. My kids thought they were great until I explained what was wrong with them."

Freddie and the Unseen World

A recent ad in a major magazine for a children's book entitled *The Door to the Secret City* described a young kid, Freddie, and his "imaginary" friend, an angel named Daniel. According to the plot, Daniel opens the door for young Freddie to visit the unseen world of nonphysical teachers who desire to be in contact with human beings. In essence this is a horrid book that encourages kids to invite demons into their lives. Yet, Pat Robertson's *Christian Broadcasting Network* (now the *Family Network*) glowingly endorsed the book, commenting: "Freddie should serve well to lift (young people) out of their problems into that wonderful dimension of imagination and make believe. What a splendid cause."[26]

The Sears Catalog and its New Age/Occult Fashion Line

The *Sears Catalog* entitled *Style--Special Edition*, dated July 31, 1988, features smiling, vigorous young girls wearing a number of T-shirts and tops with Satanic and New Age symbols. One is wearing a top with a number of squiggled Aquarius water bearer lines, upside down "6's," sun signs, and triangles (see my book *Mystery Mark of the New Age* to discover the hidden meaning of these Satanic marks).

Another little girl is pictured wearing a top printed with the word "Princess" on the front, the mark of an Indian Princess with a triangle mark on her cheek and her face separated into dark and light halves. Also observable was the occultic eagle, the sun sign, the Aquarius water bearer sign, and the crescent moon of witchcraft. The "Princess" wore seven feathers on her headdress, mimicking the number seven, the perfect number of God.

The T-shirt worn by a third young girl was equally reprehensible. Emblazoned on the front was the supposed "Peace Sign"--actually a Satanic upside down cross inside a circle, with its bars twisted downward. In occultism, the circle containing an upside down, twisted cross signifies that Satan is victorious over Jesus Christ and that he will reign forever and ever (thus the unbroken line of the circle). On the T-shirt sold by Sears, the background inside the circle was colorful and fiery. The T-shirt also displayed these telling words: "Back by Popular Demand."

Young girl's T-shirt pictured in Sears catalog.

Macy's Department Store's "New Order"

Macy's department stores in New York and California now offer a line of futuristic clothing for teens called "New Order." The stark colors of this clothing are black and white only. Inside each garment is a label permanently sewn in which reads: CONFUSION, CHAOS,

DARKNESS . . . DIRE. THEN, DESTINY'S MER-
GENCE WITH MUCH DESIRE A GRANDE
HORIZON AND EXPANDED NEW BORDER . . .
NEW ORDER

CONFUSION; CHAOS, DARKNESS
. . . DIRE.

THEN, DESTINY'S MERGENCE
WITH MUCH DESIRE

A GRANDE HORIZON AND
EXPANDED NEW BORDER

. . . NEW ORDER®

NEW
ORDER®

"clothes a girl can strut in"

USA · AUSTRALIA · LONDON · PARIS

*The label on "New Order" clothing for teenagers sold by Macy's
department stores and other outlets.*

The Baby Tapes: New Age Music for the New Being

Explorers, a company in Huntington Beach, California,
produces a product called *THE BABY TAPES: HAPPY
DREAMS.* Advertised widely, these New Age music
tapes "put your new being in touch with natural healing
and learning abilities." The manufacturer's claim is that
the audio tapes weave positive affirmations such as "I am
healthy" and "I love to learn" with special music that
affects the infant's "creative and peaceful (brain) alpha
and theta states."[27]

Unveiling the Hidden Secrets of Crystal Powers

Crystals are the "in" things for many New Agers.
Children, too, are being influenced to believe that
crystals are magical tools for self-empowerment.

In a New Age bookstore not long ago, a little child was overheard at the crystal counter begging her mother, "Please, Mommy, let me buy a power crystal." "No," her mother retorted, "you can use daddy's." "But I want *my own crystal*," the little girl pleaded.

Recently we received reports that some public elementary school teachers are having second and third graders learn simple math by using tiny crystal rocks to practice addition and subtraction. In one case, a teacher told her young students that the crystals would bring great powers from the universe into their minds and therefore help them to learn faster and better. This is just one more instance of our kids being openly taught New Age religious doctrines and practices in public schools.

The absurd notion that quartz crystals bring to their owners marvelous, positive energy forces that can somehow magically enhance learning, heal diseases, increase sexual enjoyment, or create financial prosperity is an ancient occultic teaching. In the book *Focus on Crystals,* New Age author Edmund Harold credits two "wise" spirit guides, or "illumined souls"--Christians know them as demons--for the current rage for crystals:

> The worldwide re-awakening of awareness of the benefits . . . from the use of quartz crystals is largely due to the combined efforts of two . . . illumined souls . . . Count St. Germain and the Master Djwal Khul, also known as The Tibetan Master.[28]

Not surprisingly, the demon spirit known as Count St. Germain has been identified by New Age leader Elizabeth Clare Prophet as the Hierarch, or the "Christ," of the Aquarian Age. Djwal Khul, the so-called Tibetan Master, is the same demon who dictated some 20 New Age books to Alice Bailey, late head of the Lucis Trust (former Lucifer Publishing) in New York City.

Is the New Age Behind the Plague of Illegal Drugs?

The New Age has for decades unquestionably been the major influence in the horrendous drug epidemic infecting our youth and adults. This modern plague began in earnest in the '60's with the invasion of the Hindu gurus and Eastern mysticism, invited in by such mystical rock stars as the Beatles, Cher, Bob Dylan, and the Grateful Dead. One New Age writer says that drugs became for many New Age initiates "a pass to Xanadu."[29]

The war on drugs can never be won because the powerful New Age leadership does not want to stop the spread of drugs. Psychedelic and other mind-altering drugs are the pathway to unholy trance-like meditative states for millions of today's most fervent New Age disciples. One unidentified New Ager was quoted by Marilyn Ferguson in *The Aquarian Conspiracy* as exclaiming:

> I learned from LSD about alternative realities--and suddenly all bibles made sense.[30]

While the White House encourages kids to "Just Say No!" to drugs, New Age authorities scoff and sneer and set up roadblocks to the success of the national effort. Sol Gordon, the New Age educator whose high school psychology textbook, *Psychology for You*, contains information to help kids learn about psychic powers and occultism, says the "Just Say No!" movements are "ludicrous and unworkable." Instead, what parents must do, Gordon says, is simply make kids feel good about themselves. He tells parents to improve their kids' self-esteem by *ignoring* their faults and their bad behavior.

> Parents usually list 38 things their kid is doing wrong. . . . Kids are not perfect. They make mistakes. . . . Let the whole thing go . . .[31]

The signs of the New Age promotion of mind-altering drugs are everywhere. "Cosmic Acid--Drop a Little Love" trumpets the heading in a New Age magazine advertisement. The ad offers a book by the same title, authored by a "Reverend Bill" of the Spiritual Rights Foundation, Inc. The logo for this group was also included in the ad: a half-white half-black circle with a picture of the horned devil, the all-seeing eye, the sun and stars inside the circle.

A woman from Nova Scotia, Canada, sent us a fascinatingly evil brochure published by Canada's Commission on Drug Dependency. This group is responsible for Canada's war against drugs, which is hard to believe considering the obvious Satanic symbolism on their brochure. First, I noted that the official logo for the Commission is the "X," the sign of one of the ancient Egyptian gods. The title of the brochure was, "Keep Your Dreams Alive," and the cover was embellished by three "6" shaped whirling constellations of stars: 666. In the middle of these three "6's" was one huge blazing star with streamers. The brochure announced "Drug Awareness Week" and "Communities Care."

Ecstasy: A New Transformation Drug for the New Age

New Agers are on a never-ending search for just the right drug that can bring them enlightenment and happiness. They call such drugs *transformational drugs*. It appears from press reports that the newest transformational drug of choice is a powerful, mind-warping chemical compound called *Ecstasy*.

Newsweek magazine, reporting on the explosion in numbers users of *Ecstasy*, stated:

> This is the drug that LSD was supposed to be. . . . It is called MDMA--or Ecstasy--and users say it has the incredible power to make people trust one another, to

banish jealousy, and to break down . . . barriers. . . . A
New York writer who tried it compares it to a year of
therapy in two hours.

Drug abuse clinics have begun to see kids who take a
dozen or more doses a day to achieve an Ecstasy high.
Apparently the nation is on the verge either of a
tremendous breakthrough in consciousness or a lot more
kids too strung out to come in from the rain.[32]

Underground laboratories are producing Ecstasy as
fast as it can be sold on the streets and on school campuses. New Age leaders are pushing for its legalization.
"You can say it's part of a social movement," says Rick
Doblin of Berkley's Earth Metabolic Design Foundation.[33]   As *Newsweek* concluded, Ecstasy, because it
promotes "an emotional union with the world at large," a
major New Age goal, is

. . . the drug of choice of those who identify with the
global consciousness and romantic ecology of the "New
Age Movement."[34]

Clearing Up Your Dental Karma

A number of New Age dentists across the country now
advertise that their services are designed "to help you
clear up your dental karma." In other words, your aching
tooth or crooked teeth are the result of some foul deed
you did in a previous lifetime! One Christian mother
wrote to tell me that she accidentally came across one
such dentist when she brought her child in for a dental
examination. The dentist was unknown to her but highly
recommended by a friend.

First, the unsmiling dentist's assistant explained in a
monotone, hypnotic voice that her boss' dental treatment was "holistic" in nature. Next, she informed the

mother that she could not remain present while the doctor worked on her daughter.

The mother reported that an almost overwhelming black cloud of gloominess hung over the entire dental clinic. Taken aback and nearly in a state of shock, the mother sat down in the receptionist's office and nonchalantly picked up a copy of the dentist's newsletter. There she saw it--the Satanic symbol--prominently displayed on the newsletter.

Inside the newsletter was information about how to believe in "your own personal power," mental imagery and visualization. The New Age book, *Love, Medicine, and Miracles*, by Bernie Siegel, M.D., was recommended and "Aquarian Conspirator" Marilyn Ferguson's newsletter, *The Brain/Mind Bulletin*, was cited. There was also a lot of talk about "spirit" and "wellness." Praise God, this gentle Christian woman knew what all these signs portended and so she beat a hasty retreat. In her insightful letter to me, she stated:

> So the New Age is really here and I have encountered it in all its ugliness. I am sealed with the Blessed Holy Spirit and covered in the blood of the Lamb and I was protected. How many other innocent people who go in there aren't and will be entangled in the evil web?

The Christian Response to the Rising Tide of New Age Evil

We have discussed just a few of the ways in which Satan's New Age has already infiltrated every aspect of the lives of our children. Bad already, things will surely get worse. As I explain in subsequent chapters, America is on the brink of becoming a hardened nation of devil worshipers--and kids have already begun to "trip out" on Satan.

Our Father in heaven would not have us unknowledgeable of these things, "Lest Satan should get an advantage on us: for we are not ignorant of his devices" (II Cor. 2:11). Through the discernment of the Holy Spirit and with the help of scripture, we can identify that which is New Age in origin and stay away from it. And we can protect our children. Thus, God's Word tells us to "abhor that which is evil; cleave to that which is good" (Romans 12:9).

Others in society--lukewarm or liberal "Christians" and the unsaved--will not understand nor be able to discern between good and evil. "There is a way," the Bible says, "which seemeth right unto a man but the end thereof are the ways of death" (Proverbs 14:12).

However, the prophet Daniel told us that in the last days, *God would reveal to His people the Truth* about the horrible events to transpire. He loves us and our children, and He will not leave us to perish without knowledge:

> But the wicked shall do wickedly: and none of the
> wicked shall understand, but the wise shall understand.
> (Daniel 12:10)

The New Age deception is centered on its rejection of Jesus. Even as we see the rising tide of New Age occultism all around us, let us not grow faint in our walk with Him. Our children need us. We must be of sound mind and spirit. Many now entrapped in the New Age also need us, to reach out in love and witness to them. Yes, most will reject Jesus and they will even persecute us for our testimony. Still, the New Age and all people everywhere must be told of the riches in glory obtainable only through Jesus Christ. As our Lord Himself stated:

> Whosoever therefore shall confess Me before men, him
> will I confess also before My Father which is in heaven.
> But whosoever shall deny Me before men, him will I also
> deny before My Father which is in heaven.
> (Matthew 10:32, 33)

THREE

Girl Scouts, Boy Scouts, Walt Disney, and the YWCA: The Shocking Growth of the New Age Conspiracy

But evil men and seducers shall wax worse and worse, deceiving, and being deceived. (II Tim. 3:13)

Think Globally, Act Locally.
(Girl Scout slogan, Greater
Minneapolis Girl Scout Council)

Think Globally, Act Locally.
(New Age slogan, Planetary
Initiative for the World We Choose)

Think Globally, Act Locally.
(Benjamin Ferencz and Ken Keyes, Jr.,
Planethood)

Think Globally, Act Locally.
(Donald Key, New Age organizer,
Earth at Omega)

The Boy Scouts, the Girl Scouts, Walt Disney, the YWCA, and NASA's space agency. Venerable organizations all. Who would ever believe that these bastions of society have been infiltrated and polluted with New Age teachings?

I must admit my heart has a fond place in it for the young boy or girl or teenager in a scouting uniform. When I see a youngster dressed up as a Cub Scout, Brownie, Girl Scout, or Boy Scout, my countenance automatically lightens a bit. How precious. How patriotic and touching. How wonderful. Some of my dearest friends are Scoutmasters and proud of it. Rightly so. They love their work and they love the kids under their charge. It is almost unbearable to think that Satan's New Age has made inroads in Scouting.

In exposing the astonishing headway the New Age Plan has made in scouting, and in such time-honored institutions as the YWCA, Walt Disney and NASA, we gain incredible insight into the depths to which America has sunken in embracing the wickedness of the New Age. After all, *if the Boy Scouts, the Girl Scouts, Walt Disney, the "Y", and NASA aren't off-limits to the New Age deceivers and child abusers, what or who is?*

"And now, the New Age proudly presents: Walt Disney, Michael Jackson, and Captain EO!"

Disneyland and Disneyworld. Every child dreams of one day going there in person. Their minds are flooded with pleasant and fun-filled thoughts of Mickey Mouse and Minnie Mouse, Donald Duck, Goofey, and Michael Jackson. Michael Jackson? Yes, he's there, too, starring in the New Age fantasy epic, *Captain EO*.[1]

An eighteen minute, 3-D feature spectacular, *Captain EO* is one of Disneyworld's and Disneyland's greatest and most popular attractions. But the horrible New Age imagery in this movie isn't concealed in the least. It's exploited. First, you discover that the film is playing at Disney's "Magic Eye Theatre." In the New Age religion, the magic eye, or Third Eye, is the energy point in the forehead which is supposedly opened once the person is initiated by his Master (Satan). *Captain EO* also has a logo in the form of a triangle. We know that the triangle is an occult symbol meaning the unholy trinity. It also represents the sacred sex act.

George Lucas, the director of the New Age saga *Star Wars*, produced *Captain EO* for Disney. Singer and teen heart throb, Michael Jackson, also a fervent New Ager, stars in the film, singing two of his New Age hits, "We are Here to Change the World," and "Just Another Part of Me." It's an exciting space-age adventure film for kids with such characters as a little monkey-like creature with wings, two robots, and a green elephant.

Singer Michael Jackson is "Captain EO" in Walt Disney's New Age fantasy movie produced by George Lucas.

The plot is New Age religion to the core. Blatantly so. *Captain EO* (Michael Jackson) is off to the rescue of the good queen (remarkably similar to the harlot Mystery Babylon--see Revelation 17 in the Bible) of the Black and White planet. You see, she's being held in chains because she believes in both black and white (obviously good *and* evil, right *and* wrong). Indeed, because the queen's people--everyone on the planet--believe in both black and white, they're all prisoners of "illusion." (This is the New Age/Hindu doctrine of *Maya,* or illusion--that there is really no evil in the world.)

Into the picture comes the "saviour," *Captain EO,* who dispels the "illusion" which has held the queen and her people bondage. Now, finally, they are free to believe as they wish. An unamazing, Eastern mystical end to a typical New Age plot.

During the film, moviegoers are treated to grandiose special effects. According to the official guide book, "Using the power of music, dance and light to fill the planet with all the shades of the rainbow, the EO crew overcome the evil witch by turning the . . . land into a magical world of color and happiness".[2]

The film ends gloriously with Jackson and the cast, all newly created, colorful beings, singing "We are here to change the world!"

Disney's Contributions to the New Age

The Disney amusement centers have done great things to please the New Age lord of enchantment. Disneyworld's Epcot Center has its "Journey into Imagination," a pavilion constructed with the New Age symbolism of mind--imposing triangles of glass and two towering pyramids.

Throughout Disneyworld, including Epcot Center, the kids will discover shops and exhibits with such New Age symbols and idols as unicorns, wizards, crystals, and rainbows proudly displayed. There's also the opportunity to visit the mythical New Age Isle of Atlantis on a submarine tour. The "It's a Small World" show takes kids on a boat cruise to be taught one-worldism, while the

"Haunted Mansion" whirls kids into the realm of ghosts and monsters.

For many years, Disney has alternately presented fine movies and entertainment for kids mixed with entertainment deceptively laced and impregnated with dangerous New Age mysticism. The *Hobbit*, a wizards and sorcery "delight," is featured on Cable TV's Disney channel, which is advertised as the channel that will "fill your house with magic."

Walt Disney's very first major movie production, 1940's *Fantasia*, is a psychedelic extravaganza which the New Age dearly loves. It's been rereleased to widespread acclaim. The mystical music in *Fantasia* is also a treat to New Agers, including selections from the Satanist/anarchist pagan composer, Igor Stravinsky.

David Tame, author of *The Secret Power of Music*, a New Age book/essay on music, raves about this early Disney New Age production:

> For anybody who hasn't seen it, this 1940 Disney production is a must. A superb marriage between the visual and musical arts. Most of the sequences . . . are what New Age cinema was intended to be![3]

Walt Disney's immoral motto seems to be "give 'em whatever will sell!" What will sell includes a two hour special feature cartoon on Valentine's Day--set to the hard rock music of *Madonna*, *Prince*, and *The Rolling Stones*--and a recent showing of an adventure tale in which Unico the unicorn visits a magical island and makes friends with the devil there.

Later, in Chapter 10, "Satan's Bookshelf," we'll examine another of Disney's more dismal unholy projects: Mickey Mouse in the role of "The Sorcerer's Apprentice."

Boy Scouts, Girl Scouts, and the New Age

The Boy Scouts of America (BSA) and Girl Scouts of America (GSA) alike are experiencing change due to New Age pressures. And not changes for the better, either. Shocking New Age practices, beliefs, and symbols have in recent years been adopted and are today being defended by the national leadership of these once honorable and impeccable scouting institutions.

The steady demise of the Boy Scouts was hastened about two years ago when the BSA caved in to a lawsuit by the parents of a 15-year-old atheist and removed language from its program and literature that defines God as a Supreme Being. Following on the heels of this horrible and grievous mistake in judgment, the BSA buckled under to disgruntled radical feminists and agreed to allow women to become scout-masters.[4]

It is sad to see a group such as the Boy Scouts that could be used for such holy purposes diminish so rapidly in godly stature. Another indication, however, of the fading worth of the Boy Scouts can be found within the pages of its popular *Boy's Life* magazine. One article, for example, carried a "health" article entitled "What is Yoga?" Yoga was defined in the article as "a set of ancient poses and exercises that stretch the muscles, strengthen the body, and discipline the mind." The author strongly advised young readers to practice yoga. Once yoga becomes your sport, he wrote, "you will find it a good tool for dealing with whatever challenges--mental or physical--come along."[5]

In fact, yoga is *not* a sport nor a benign exercise program. It is a worship ritual of the Hindu and New Age religion. Yoga, which means "to become yoked with" is designed to link one's mind, spirit, and body with the gods and, ultimately, the "Infinite One." The youngster who practices yoga must contort the body into a number of Satanic shapes and images, including the cobra serpent, pyramid or triangle, assorted occultic "power animals" (such as the lion of the god Mithra) and demonic gargoyles.[6]

Rarely are the young person and his parents aware that yoga is the unholy ritual of an evil religion and that the body of the yoga devotee' actually becomes shaped as an accursed Satanic symbol.

This is the secret that yoga teachers and New Age planners do not want the public to discover. But a brief look at what these individuals *tell each other* in their numerous religious journals and books will prove the blackened spiritual origins and nature of yoga. For example, in *Yoga Journal,* George Feurstein states, "From study one should proceed to practice yoga. . . . The Supreme Self is revealed through perfection in study and practice."[7] Moreover, Feurstein affirms that:

> The principal scripture of pre-classical yoga is the widely read *Bhagavad-Gita,* which is the 'New Testament of Hinduism.' Few people know that it is traditionally considered to be . . . a secret doctrine that has been revealed, rather than authored by a human individual.[8]

Regardless of its Hindu/New Age connection, yoga is now commonly required at a number of elementary, junior high and high schools throughout America. It is also offered through courses of instruction at community health and recreation centers, at YWCA centers, and elsewhere.

The Girl Scouts of America: Secretly a Pawn of the New Age?

It is apparent that the New Age has infiltrated and tainted the Girl Scouts even more so than the Boy Scouts. Signs of this are rampant. Most evident are the New Age and occultic symbols on the uniform patches and badges for Girl Scout troops. Recently a young girl active in scouting took her newest catalog list of patches and badges to her mother and said, "Look, Mom, these are the same as the occult symbols and marks described and shown in Texe Marrs' book, *Mystery Mark of the New Age*." Aghast, her mother sent the catalog, along with a letter expressing her dismay, to my ministry.

Frankly, when I examined the detailed features of the badges and patches illustrated in the catalog, I, too, was aghast. Someone at the top levels of Girl Scouting is making a bold and determined effort to condition our kids' minds with some of the most hideous signs ever devised by Satan's agents. To think that tens of thousands of intense, dedicated, and innocent young girls are unknowingly wearing these patches and badges on their uniforms! It's unthinkable. It's terrible. And it's unconscionable.

Among the worst of the Girls Scout patches are these:

Visual Arts Patch. Has the all-seeing eye of Horus the Egyptian Sun God inside a circle with six colorful rainbow rays radiating outward from the eye. In the New Age, the rainbow symbolizes the *rainbow bridge*--man's bridge, or pathway, to becoming his own god. This is a perversion of God's rainbow which he gave to man as a sign of His covenant with us (see Genesis 9:13).

Tune in to Well Being. Depicts a child, arms lifted, atop a triangle. Inside the torso of the child is yet another triangle. The triangle is a Satanic sign indicating, among other things, belief in the *unholy trinity* of Egyptian and Babylonian gods and goddesses and also the trinity of man (mind, body, spirit). It does not, as some suppose, stand for God's Holy Trinity.

Global Understanding. A circle atop a circle (the globe) to indicate oneness with the world, or all is divine, all is one.

New Age occult symbolism has made its way into Girl Scouting through proficiency badges, interest project patches, and insignia for uniforms.

Dabbler. The Girl Scouting organization offers four different "dabbler" patches. In each, the globe is the most prominent feature. One shows a person with lifted hands and spread-eagled legs against a backdrop of blue earth and the sun's rays. In the occult world, this means oneness with the planetary forces.

American Indian Lore. The Indian Medicine Man and Shaman is revered by New Agers for his earth magic incantations and for his ability to communicate with and obtain assistance from the spirit realm. This patch, with its symbolic mosaic, gives credence to this New Age belief.

Managing Stress. The scene on this patch is of the sun at dawn, presiding over a placid and peaceful stream of water. Under the guise of reducing and managing stress, our children are increasingly being subjected to visualization, meditation, deep breathing, and other occult techniques and exercises.

The section in the Scouting manual which describes the meaning and significance of this patch could only have been written by someone who has conducted an in-depth study of New Age methods and techniques. The author recommends girls "listen to a variety of types of music and find pieces that evoke different emotions in you--happiness, sorrow, anger, playfulness, etc."[9]

The way to practice New Age visualization is minutely described and the reader is told to "find a cassette tape with a recorded relaxation exercise on it that you can use." Nature or environmental sounds are especially recommended. The instructions do not warn, however, that almost all such tapes include New Age "mood" music--a form of hypnotic, trance-inducing music designed to send the person's mind into an altered state of consciousness, inviting in demonic entities.

The manual also includes deep, rhythmic breathing exercises and chanting techniques designed to send a person into a trance-like, vegetative state of nothingness so demons can enter.[10]

My World in My Community. This badge is blatantly New Age. It is the yin/yang symbol--a circle split into two halves by a Satanic "S" that crookedly snakes its way from top to bottom. Each side therefore resembles the number 6 (see Rev. 13 for the prophecy of the Beast with the number 666). Inside each "6" is the sun god dot, or point, of Lucifer.

The Girl Scouts "The World in My Community" proficiency badge is the yin-yang occult symbol so prevalent among Eastern religions.

The yin/yang is a mystical oriental sign extremely popular in Confuciusism, Taoism, Buddhism, and other Eastern religions. It stands for the integrating, or mixture, of light and dark, good and evil, male and female.

The official *Girl Scout Handbook* teaches young readers many of the same principles about *Community* that hard-core New Age advocates are teaching. These principles are in hostile opposition to patriotism and Christianity.

First Aid. This badge consists of the Maltese Cross, a perverted cross composed of four triangles, each having its apex facing the direction of the center. The cross is contained within a red circle border.

Personal Health. Again we find the red circle border and inside is the ancient Tau cross, indicative of the cross, or tree, on which Jesus hung, but placed upside down for mockery.

Math Whiz. A "happy face" on a red triangle.

New Brownie Girl Scout "Try-Its" badges are all shaped as triangles. Note the rainbow sun rays of the "Girl Scouts Ways" badge (right).

The new "Bridge to Adult" Girl Scout insignia is a triangle-shaped rainbow. The New Age religion claims the rainbow symbolizes man's "bridge to godhood."

Try-Its. Five series of three badges, fifteen in all, the Try-Its are all shaped in the form of triangles. Among the Try-Its with occultic overtones is the "Science Magic" badge and the "Girl Scout Ways" badge. The latter badge depicts six colorful, rainbow-like sun rays.

"Think Globally, Act Locally"—a New Age Slogan for the Girl Scouts

The Greater Minneapolis Girl Scout Council has a patch that says "Think Globally, Act Locally." This slogan is not unique. It is one of the most cherished in the New Age movement. It was the heralded cry for the Planetary Congress held in Toronto, Canada, in 1983. The theme for that Congress, in which many of the world's top New

Age globalist leaders and most of the major groups and organizations participated, was "Think Globally, Act Locally."[11] It is also a slogan popularized by the powerful New Age organization, Planetary Initiative for the World We Choose.[12]

To "Think Globally, Act Locally" means that the New Age disciple is to visualize and work for a unique one world system--a one world religion, a one world government, a one world economy. To achieve this unity of all mankind--so that the planet and man collectively become divine--disciples are to "Act Locally." In other words, to be local activists, supporting the Global New Age Plan and agenda by all means possible. The peace movement, disarmament, the environment, and globalism issues are paramount.

Who is Behind this Slogan?

Donald Key, in his important New Age book, *Earth at Omega*, identified a number of high echelon New Age organizations that are behind the networking movement to Think Globally, Act Locally:

> The original inviters of the Planetary Initiative were the leaders of the Association for Humanistic Psychology, the Club of Rome, Global Education Associates, the United Nations Association . . . and of course, Planetary Citizens.[13]

In their peace-propaganda book, *Planethood: The Key to Your Survival and Prosperity*, Benjamin Ferencz, Adjunct Professor of International Law at Pace University, and Ken Keyes, Jr., New Age author and United Nations lobbyist, set forth a blueprint for the establishment of a one-world government. They reveal that the magical phrase "Think Globally, Act Locally" is the essential catalyst that can propel the planet toward a one world order. "Think globally, act locally," Ferencz and Keyes encourage readers. "It's up to you! You can empower yourself to save the world."[14]

It is therefore not an accident that the Girl Scouts of Minneapolis have adopted the New Age slogan, "Think Globally, Act Locally." The national headquarters of the Girl Scouts of America has implemented a whole new series of projects called "Global Understanding." The motto that was printed on their scout leader books, naturally, is "Think Globally, Act Locally."[15]

Who is responsible for this abomination? Well, contemplate this: Orville Freeman, former U.S. Secretary of Agriculture in the ultra-liberal Carter administration, is on the Board of Directors of *The Futurist*, a magazine published by the influential New Age-oriented organization, The World Future Society. The World Future Society is a major promoter and sponsor of one-worldism projects. *Orville Freeman's wife is president of the Girl Scouts of America.*[16]

Back to Minneapolis for More New Age Propaganda

The Greater Minneapolis Girl Scout Council expresses in its official pamphlet many of the same goals as the other New Age groups (note particularly key words and phrases such as "peace," "all nations and cultures," "network," and "universal"):

> Girl Scouting is in a unique position to promote communication, understanding, and peace among nations and cultures. The combined effort and leadership from the Girl Scout Network will have a positive impact on such universal problems as literacy, hunger, health care and preservation of natural resources.[17]

Naturally, it is a good and commendable thing for Girl Scouts to be encouraged by their leaders to become involved in such worthy endeavors as ending world hunger, protecting the environment, and solving the literary problem. However, it is a wicked thing to attempt to do so under the umbrella and leadership mantle of New Age organizations and men and women whose true, but veiled and unacknowledged, goal is not to accomplish all these noteworthy objectives but instead to desecrate our God and destroy our kids in the process.

The sinister New Age humanist agenda of the Greater Minneapolis Girl Scout Council becomes even more crystal clear when we read in the same Girl Scout brochure how the contributions of Girl Scout supporters may be used. A contribution in the amount of $25, says the brochure, "provides a troop program on healthy male/female relationships and pregnancy prevention."[18] Considering the New Age views of the Council's leadership, we can be quite positive that sexual abstinence was not what the brochure has in mind when it refers to such sex education programs.

New Age at the "Y"

Judging from complaints we are receiving from Christian parents, nationally the Young Women's Christian Association (YWCA) is fast becoming a hotbed of New Age activity.

In a recent issue of the excellent *Christian Information Bureau (CIB) Newsletter*, the editor despairingly wrote, "If you still do not understand the New Age movement, perhaps you could pick up some courses at the YWCA in Reno, Nevada. Their catalog's table of contents yields a potpourri of New Age teachings."[19] Then followed a list of the various course titles offered by the "Y" of Reno. They included Hatha Yoga, Meditation, and Tai Chi under the title, "Exercises for Holistic

Health." Also offered: Tibetan Chanting, Kahuna (Hawaiian spirits' teachings), and The Healing Path of a Shaman. Movies available under the topic "Films for a New Age," included *Towards New Communities in the New World* and *Expanding Consciousness.*

Joining Forces with the Devil

There were at the Reno YMCA, in addition, films on Jung, psychology, supermemory, the I Ching divination system, mysticism, Taoism, Zen Buddhism, right brain/ left brain theory, dream therapy and self-esteem, and on and on. But, in the entire YWCA course catalog *there was not one mention of Christianity. Not one.* The *CIB* editor's conclusion was therefore most appropriate: "They should change their name," he said, "to the YWOA (Young Women's Occult Association)."[20]

NASA'S Space Program and the New Age

NASA, overseer of America's space program, has had its spectacular successes and also a number of monumental failures. But judging from its recent embracing of the New Age, the problems have only begun. Eerie indications are that NASA's highest level managers are deeply involved in the New Age religion. *The Wall Street Journal* reported that the space agency paid Werner Erhard, guru of the discredited New Age training program, EST and founder of a similar new program, The Forum, $45,000 to *personally* train a group of its top executives. Erhard's program has been called a blend of "business focused Zen (Buddhism), Scientology, and Gestalt."[21]

Kids greatly admire NASA and the astronauts are considered as heroes. But regrettably, at least one astronaut, Edgar Mitchell, has become an evangelist for the New Age and is a very poor role model.

The New Age infiltration of NASA's space program has shown up in its official patches, sold to kids to wear on their clothing. Among the New Age occultic symbols used by NASA: the triple circle within the triangle (the number "3" has great occult significance), man inside three rainbow circles; the red sun god; the "X;" three blazing streaks encircled that form a star; pegasus horses with the sun sign; the "Sun God" face; the ghost eagle; the infinity 8; the sign of Mars, god of war; and the sign of man inside a circle comprised of half day and half night.

*NASA patches for kids are loaded with
occultic symbols and meaning.*

Only art designers with a keen knowledge of occult, pagan, and gnostic symbolism--or designers occultly led by demons with such knowledge--could have come up with these sinister patches.

Satan "Preaches" to Kids in Some "Christian" Churches

As the example of the YWCA demonstrates, the New Age leadership is not deterred by the term "Christian." There can be no question that the absolutely worst cases of New Age child abuse are those that are increasingly occurring in our Christian churches.

Earlier I mentioned the startling inclusion of New Age symbols and concepts in some of our Sunday School curricula. Even more alarming are the many instances of blatant, outright occultism we have discovered. A prime example comes from the First Christian Church in Boulder, Colorado. That church's youth group distributed a *Boulder Free School* newsletter describing such course offerings as Kundalini Yoga, Visualization, Tai Chi Chuan, Tarot Cards and Astrology for Teenagers, Basic Metaphysics, Spirit Channeling, and A Survey of New Age Thought.[22] This from a "Christian" church!

Regrettably, I could fill up the pages of an entire separate book describing such horrors occurring in churches across America. The pastors and youth leaders involved are either *not* Christian or they pitifully need to pray for discernment. Until these pastors accept Jesus as Lord and Savior and are born again into His Kingdom (see John 3:3), or until they repent and seek greater discernment, my ministry will continue to be besieged by such reports as the following:

● A Lutheran pastor who allowed the high school youth to present a program to the entire church introducing them to the occultic-laced fantasy game, *Dungeons & Dragons*.

● The charismatic pastor of one of Oklahoma's largest churches whose church bookstore sells locally-made T-shirts with a picture of a bloody sword on the front and the caption: "Take the Kingdom by Violence." (This quote is taken out of context from Matthew 11:12 where Jesus actually denounces those rebels who wrongly attempt to bring in the Kingdom of Heaven by unrighteous violence and force.)

● In 1988, at America's largest Cathedral, the Episcopal Cathedral of St. John the Divine in New York City, the pastor, Rev. James Parks Morton, conducted a Thanksgiving Day service in which 4,000 children and adults joined with American Indians, tribal leaders, medicine men, witches, nature worshipers and other anti-Christian elements in a "Circle dance" of religious friendship and unity. Morton said the purpose of the dance was to "redefine" Thanksgiving. He also declared that part of the impetus for the ceremony was to create "a heightened consciousness of the necessity of different religions working together to save our planet."[23]

● In the Orlando, Florida area, for the Christmas season a Baptist pastor refused to put up the traditional Jesus in a manger scene on the church lawn. Instead, he put on display a lighted, life-size, blue plastic "The Smurfs" scene. Later in this book, I'll demonstrate the occultism so evident in the popular *Smurfs* TV series for kids. Obviously, this pastor has lost sight of "The reason for the season"--Jesus Christ, and he is promoting worldly secular values to his congregation. What a horrid example for the world to see as autos drive by a church and the occupants view the unholy Smurfs display.

● At a number of recent Catholic youth retreats and conferences, nuns and priests taught the children Zen

Buddhism, "Creation-centered spirituality," yoga, Jungian meditation, and self-love.

● An article by Rev. S. Wesley Ariarajah, a director of the World Council of Churches (WCC), helps us to understand how pastors, youth directors and other local church leaders are going astray and becoming front men and women for Satan's New Age assault on our kids. The World Council of Churches and its twin in evil works, the National Council of Churches (NCC), are both strongly supported by such evangelical ecumenical leaders as John Stott and Billy Graham. Yet, their pro-New Age, anti-Jesus bias and bigotry is rudely apparent in almost every publication and bulletin the WCC and NCC release.

Reverend Ariarajah's article in an issue of the *International Christian Digest* reveals this ungodly and regrettable attitude and doctrine. In answering the question, "Is Jesus the *Only Way*?," the apostate Ariarajah, basing his answers on the World Council of Churches' *The Bible and People of Other Faiths*, heretically writes:

> Jesus makes no claims to divinity or to oneness with God. He does not suggest himself to be a mediator, much less the only mediator between God and men. Thus, can a Christian turn around and say to the Buddhist that he or she is misguided? . . . We have no grounds to do so.[24]

This is simply another gospel and another Jesus. The Apostle Paul told us there would be "accursed" heretics like these coming forth with their Satanic gospels (Galatians 1:8). Unfortunately, our kids are learning these false gospels of the New Age as they attend Sunday Schools and sit in the pews and listen to Satanic lies and blasphemies against our Lord Jesus Christ spread by New Age ministers of unrighteousness who come cloaked as

"Christian" pastors, reverends, priests, youth directors, and Sunday School teachers.

The reason for the New Age assault on our churches is understandable. Satan's New Age has discovered the ultimate key to capturing the soul of a child. Above all, the child's spiritual foundation must be built on the lie that Jesus is not Saviour and Lord. The unholy goal is to bring children into darkness, therefore, *first you must destroy their faith in Jesus.*

First, You Destroy Their Faith in Jesus

And they brought young children to Him, that He should touch them; and His disciples rebuked those that brought them. But when Jesus saw it, He was much displeased, and said unto them, "Suffer the little children to come unto Me, and forbid them not: for of such is the kingdom of God." (Mark 10:13, 14)

Jesus of Nazareth prepared for many lives for his incarnation as a world teacher. . . . After Jesus' death his followers started to insist that only he was the Son of God and that people could only be saved by believing in him. White Eagle (my teacher) has a slightly different interpretation: that people are saved by. . . . the light within them. . . . Jesus himself did not mean for people to worship him.

(Jenny Dent
Spiritual Teaching for Children Series)

Take *just one generation* of children, carefully mix a brew of unholy and intellectual poison, feed their young, impressionable minds the spiritual lie that Jesus is not Lord and Savior and that the Bible is not the true and complete Word of God--presto! You have the dawning of a New Age. This is the diseased but cunning goal of Satan. His campaign to destroy the faith of the young in Jesus perfectly expresses the very essence of his ungodly

Plan to ravage our kids. With Jesus in their hearts, the Evil Master of the New Age cannot touch even a hair of our precious childrens' heads. Cruelly take Jesus away, leave the kids without hope and without a reason for living, and they become vulnerable, defenseless and lost. They are ripe for the taking.

Traits of Children

Without a caring Christian environment in which the child is taught about the pure things of God, he or she easily falls prey to evil. Innocent little children have a simple faith. They want to believe whatever an authority tells them and will usually believe what they are told with little argument and debate. With a freshness and newness of spirit they place their total trust in the adults over them. Jesus our Lord was well aware of this and He was also aware of the danger to children of men full of Satan who despise and plot their destruction.

> Take heed that ye despise not one of these little ones; for I say unto you, that in heaven their angels do always behold the face of my Father which is in heaven. For the Son of man is come to save that which was lost. . . . Even so it is not the will of your Father which is in heaven, that one of these little ones should perish.
>
> (Matthew 18:10, 11, 14)

Childhood An Opportunity for Satan's New Agers

The innocence of the young, and their unsophistication and trusting nature, give Satan's New Age clique the opportunity they desire to attack and destroy. Raised to love God and His Son Jesus Christ and to honor and revere His Word, our children grow to become godly, kind, and strong in temperament and spirit. Christian parents who teach their young to hunger and thirst for the fruits of the Spirit will experience an overwhelming positive response. These fruits of the Spirit are outlined in Galatians 5:22, 23 and include love, joy, peace, patience, gentleness, goodness, faith and meekness. Children raised on these fruits will be a blessing to parents in their declining years.

The New Age, however, offers a far different mode of child raising. Children are to be raised to attune themselves to despicable demon spirits (disguised as "angels of light"). They are instructed to blasphemously consider themselves "little gods," to value self-love and narcissism more than the love of God, to consider self-esteem more important than loving one's neighbor, to disrespect and hold Jesus Christ up to scorn, to trust in their own intuition rather than the Word of God, to believe in the false gods and deceitful doctrines of the Hindu and other mystical religions, and to dishonor church and country while exalting the global "Community" and the oneness of mankind.

New Age Doctrines Weaken the Child's Character

Fed a steady diet of New Age lies, children soon become hardened to the truth and diseased in body, soul, and mind. Deprived of the knowledge and wisdom that would lead them to God, young people can little withstand the lure of the flesh. Trained to love self, to "do as thou wilt," and to ridicule the "preposterous" notion that Jesus is *the Way*, the child as he matures as a teenager and into adulthood is irresistibly drawn into unholy thoughts and unseemly behavior. Paul gave us, in Galatians 5:19-21, a catalog of these evil works of the flesh:

Now the works of the flesh are manifest, which are these, adultery, fornication, uncleanness, lasciviousness,

idolatry, witchcraft, hatred, variance, emulations,
wrath, strife, seditions, heresies, envyings, murders,
drunkenness, revelings, and such like. . . .

Those who practice these vile things, God warns, will
not enter the Kingdom of Heaven (Gal. 5:21); yet, New
Age religious teachings--coming into childrens' minds
like a flood today--inevitably and inexorably so weaken a
child's character that he or she becomes utterly helpless
when the most repugnant and revolting of temptations
come. Again, the key is Jesus. He is the shield, the
armor, the refuge of strength that is denied children by
the New Age.

New Age on the Rampage

There still remains a lot of confusion today regarding the
very term "New Age." What does it all mean? How can a
person best understand the meaning of the New Age
movement and religion? If we are to protect our
children, we first need to understand the forces that seek
their destruction.

Briefly, but accurately stated, the New Age is an
anything but Jesus religion. Satan is not a finicky and
particular master. He well knows that the only trick he
needs to perform to conquer a person's soul is that of
separating the individual from the powerful and merciful
love of Jesus.

Yes, the New Age landscape is littered with bizarre
rituals, idolatry, ideas and concepts, and teachings.
Among these we find reincarnation, fantasy books and
games (e.g., Dungeons and Dragons, Nintendo's *Wizards
and Warriors*), white magic, black magic, sorcery, shamanism, polytheism (multiple gods and goddesses),
occult symbols (the swastika, pentagram, circle, triangle,
unicorn, etc.), holistic medicine (polarity therapy,
acupuncture, reflexology, rebirthing), physical tests and

sports (Ninja, the martial arts, yoga, etc.), occult objects and idols (occult figurines, crystals, pyramids, etc.), psychology (visualization, meditation, healing of memories), UFO's and extraterrestrials, witchcraft and satan worship, astrology and the horoscope, tarot card reading, ouija boards, palm readings, fire-walking, seances, mediums and spirit channeling. All these and more are signs of New Age occultism and influence in the world.

The most sinister and dangerous aspect of the New Age, as far as our kids are concerned, is that all of these occultic rituals, beliefs, practices, artifacts, and objects often are presented to children in glittery, attractive spiritual wrappings. The New Age leadership has placed top priority on the religious education of kids in an all out effort to reorient their worldview away from Jesus and Christianity.

The Spiritual Initiation of Kids

Satan reasons that if their parents can be reached first, kids will accept the New Age worldview easily and without question. To achieve Satan's goal of a totally New Age society devoid of even a trace of faith in Jesus, his New Age disciples have developed a number of tools to assist parents to *initiate* their helpless and captive children into the New Age spirituality. Such tools include New Age home learning textbooks and study manuals, Sunday School lesson curricula to fit New Age criteria and doctrine, parenting and psychology self-help books, parenting magazines and newsletters, and New Age conferences, seminars, and workshops for parents.

One mind-boggling example is a set of four religious instruction books designed for kids and published by The White Eagle Publishing Trust in England. Written and developed by Jenny Dent, they are widely distributed in America through New Age bookstores and by mail.

Entitled "The Spiritual Teaching for Children Series," these four books are jam-packed with teachings on reincarnation, demon spirit channeling, astral travel, Eastern religions and other New Age themes.[1] Attractively packaged, the books are also loaded with occult symbols.

The SPIRITUAL TEACHING FOR CHILDREN SERIES *instructs children on New Age religious concepts.*

We get the first glint of impending horror from merely examining the covers of these four books. Each depicts a young boy or girl of about seven or eight years old sitting in a lotus-like Hindu meditation pose. On three of the books' covers, the child is framed by a hexagram star and a wheel (the Hindu symbol of recycling and reincarnation).

Then comes the next clue to the dangers to children that lie within the pages of these glossy, expensively produced "spiritual teaching" guides. In the introduction, author Jenny Dent proudly tells parents that she owes a deep debt of gratitude to her spirit guide and teacher, *White Eagle*. It is he, she reveals, who inspired publication of the books:

> My Teacher, White Eagle, has helped me understand the truth and beauty in every religion and pathway to God, and he teaches the Ancient Wisdom with fresh insight for the New Aquarian Age. I have known and loved White Eagle since childhood (and in many past lives I believe). He did not come back to earth this time in a physical body. . . . White Eagle used the personality of an American Indian Chief of the Iroquois tribe and we can learn much from the American Indians and their way of life and spiritual knowledge.
>
> But now, in this New Age, a very special part of White Eagle's teaching is to help us to use our inner light, the part of God, the Christ within the heart (the Atman). . . .[2]

From Generation to Generation New Age Teachings Spread

In another revealing comment, author Dent also acknowledges the contribution of her grandmother, Grace, who first opened up to the spirit known as "White Eagle" and of her mother, Joan, "for awakening my understanding of spiritual truth from earliest childhood, and for the example she set in starting our work with children in the White Eagle Lodge." The White Eagle Lodge, Dent goes on to explain, is a New Age church first begun by her grandmother.[3]

Sadly we see here the accumulated spiritual poison of the New Age over a span of three generations. Demonic teachings, invited in by a grandmother, were transmitted and eventually infected the mother and then the daughter. Perhaps a fourth generation in this same family is even now being introduced to the occult teachings of the New Age as the harvest cycle of error and evil continues to ferment and ripen.

Spiritual Teachings for Children in the New Age

Dent recommends that parents sit down with their children and over time patiently work through each of the four books consecutively since, together, they constitute a basic curricula to teach the child the spiritual "truths" of the New Age. Here are a few prime examples of what children are to be taught. As you read, try to put yourself in the child's place. Imagine yourself as a little, trusting, open child eagerly looking forward to being taught by mommy or daddy of these great, wonderful spiritual truths. These are the kinds of things you will be taught.

Volume 1, GOD LOVES US ALL

In Volume 1, *God Loves Us All*, the child is led in a meditation exercise, being told, "Now take a deep breath and imagine you are breathing in the sunlight. . . . You are breathing in God's love and light and life-force."[4] Also, there is instruction on Mother God and on the New Age belief in the sun god: "Our Creator must be a mother, too, for we all need a mother. . . . Think of Father God as being the sun . . . and Mother God as being like the earth."[5]

This New Age belief in the Sun as Father God and the Earth as Mother God is of pagan origins. It is the same doctrine of creation worship taught in the old Mystery Religions, which the Apostle Paul (Romans 1:21, 22) identified as anti-God:

> Because that, when they knew God, they glorified Him not as God, neither were thankful, but became vain in their imaginations and their foolish heart was darkened. Professing themselves to be wise they became fools . . .

Dent also teaches the child that Mother God is symbolized by a circle with a point inside (actually an ancient occultic sign for Lucifer--the point of light within the sun).[6] Finally, the child is told:

> Mother God is often called Divine Mother and we can picture her also as a beautiful woman. She is close to all women, especially mothers, and helps them to be wise and loving with her children. She is close to all children too, and will help and comfort you if you feel unhappy.[7]

In reality, though this *Spiritual Teaching for Children* book does not admit it, what it is alluding to here is the ancient Mother Goddess figure. In Revelation 17, our Bible describes this false goddess as the harbinger of Satan's last days One World Religion. Her Name: "Mystery Babylon, Mother of Harlots and Abominations of the Earth."

In contrast to the New Age teaching, Jesus is the *only* mediator between man and God (I Tim. 2:5), and He sits at the right hand of the Father. There is no Mother Goddess in heaven. Therefore, the Mother of the New Age is, in fact, "Satan's Mistress"--the harlot church symbolized as Mystery Babylon.

Everyone is "Christ"

This same Volume 1 also presents a false concept of
Christ and the Holy Spirit to children and promotes Eastern mystical religions as equal in stature to Christianity:

> The part of God in *all* people is like a little light shining
> in the heart. Some people call this the "Christ," while
> others use different names: for example, in Yoga
> teaching it is called "the Aturan." *It shines in people who
> believe in God and people who do not.* . . . . It shines in
> people who call themselves Christians or Buddhists or
> Muslims or Hindus or any religious name.

> It does not matter what we believe or do we are all part
> of God's great family and He loves us all.[8]

Volume 2, WHERE IS HEAVEN?

"Where is heaven?" Volume 2 asks. The New Age
answer: heaven is simply the spirit world where the
angels and other discarnate souls without bodies live.
God is not there, since there is no personal God. The
spirit of "Jesus" does reside in the New Age version of
heaven children learn; but, in contrast to what the Bible
teaches, the New Age Jesus does not sit on a throne. And
he's not in charge of heaven. *He's merely one of many
spirits.* Furthermore, children are also told they can
merge and communicate with these spirits:

> Where is heaven? Is it far away above the clouds? No,
> heaven is not right up in the sky . . . it is all around us. . . .
> We can all tune into the heaven world in our meditation
> time.[9]

> When we go to sleep at night we leave our earthly body
> and go into our body of light in the heaven world . . . we
> remember some things about our time in the heaven

world and the people there . . . including perhaps someone we love whose earth body has died.[10]

Continuing, Dent tells kids the New Age lie that each child is assigned a "spirit guide" or "teacher" from the "Heaven World" to be his lifelong companion and aide. This is an amazing attempt to camouflage demon spirits, either as friendly and helpful guardian "angels" or as watchful, protective spirits of the deceased residing in "heaven." These spirits, Volume 2 teaches, have chosen this helping role rather than to reincarnate into other bodies.

Volume 3, THE GIANT JIGSAW

Volume 3 of Jenny Dent's *Spiritual Teachings for Children* series is worse than Volumes 1 and 2, if this is possible.

On page 7 is a meditation exercise designed to help the child have an out-of-body experience, also known as *astral travel.* On page 8, the subject turns to *reincarnation,* teaching that people are born over and over and that there is no heaven as Christians foolishly believe. Heaven is simply the Spirit World.

> Life on earth is rather like being at school. When the term ends we take off our school uniform (the earth body) and have a vacation, a holiday in the heaven world, where we rest and get ready for another term on earth.

> We are not forced to come back to earth but eventually, after . . . being shown lessons we didn't learn too well in our past lives, we *ask* to come back to get on with our work--(just as you are glad to get back to school after a holiday).[11]

Is Sexual Abuse Implicitly Encouraged?

The volatile and sinister aspect of the *reincarnation doctrine* that breeds *child sexual abuse and incest* is also emphasized. For example, kids are instructed that:

> In families, a mother and son might be husband and wife in another life, or brother and sister; we can change our sex in different lives. . . .[12]

The evil New Age doctrine of reincarnation is soundly rejected by scripture. As we read in Hebrews 9:27: "It is appointed for a man once to die, afterward the judgment." But to an adult who does not want to be judged by an Almighty God whom he or she has rejected and perhaps blasphemed and ridiculed, reincarnation is not only convenient, it is cunningly comforting. This is one of Satan's smoothest lies--that man does not have to face judgment and the sure wrath of the God whom he has spurned. No, you will live forever, cycle after cycle, the Father of Liars whispers in the ears of his New Age disciples, until you become as the gods.

The Easy Death Doctrine of the New Age

Reincarnation is an especially damaging lie in relation to kids. A tragic and grotesque example of this came to light not long ago in Oklahoma. According to news reports, a young 13-year-old girl took a box of matches from the kitchen, a can of gasoline from the garage, and quietly went upstairs to her little brother's bedroom. There he lay peacefully taking a nap. The girl carefully poured the gasoline on the floor all around the bed and soaked the bedding for good measure. Then she calmly lit a match and attempted to burn her own little brother to death.[13]

Later, the young girl tearfully told police investigators that she had not realized that she was really hurting her little brother. She had been told all about reincarnation and believed in it. Her brother had been complaining a lot recently, she added, and so she decided to go ahead and send him to "heaven"--the spirit world--where he would be given a new body in which to reincarnate. "I thought he would be more happy if he could be born into another family or come back as something he would enjoy," she explained.[14]

Satan's despicable teachings on reincarnation are perfectly--if cruelly--designed to fascinate and enthrall the minds of adventurous youth. Kids are naturally curious and imaginative. They want to learn all about kings and queens, wizards, knights, warriors, and heros and heroines of long ago. They become excited and gleeful when they hear delightful tales of princes and princesses, of "Once Upon a Time."

What a grand opportunity for Satan! To really captivate (and capture) kids' breathlessly expectant and absorbent minds, he has his New Age disciples on earth sit a little boy or girl down and say, "Once upon a time, you were a knight at King Arthur's roundtable," or . . . an Indian chief, an Austrian princes, a heroic Viking, an Egyptian priestess, a famous president, a glamorous movie actress." As Dent exclaims to kids:

> I wonder who I was before. We all have had many lives,
> sometimes rich and famous. . . . Can you think of a
> different nationality you would like to have been in a
> past life or a particular job you would like to have done,
> like helping to build the Great Pyramid?[15]

Defaming Jesus: The Bizarre Tale of Harry and Crispin

However, as insidious as the teaching of reincarnation is, by far the most hideous section in Volume 3 does not deal with reincarnation, but with the deceitful and despicable way in which Jesus Christ is presented. This section involves Dent offering a picture of two kids, one good and loving and kind, the other cruel, mean, and selfish. The first is named Harry Happyheart. Harry, explains the author, "is sowing lots of kind, loving, thoughtful seeds." Kids are then invited to use crayons or color marking pens to draw in the *beautiful plants* into which the seeds of Harry Happyheart will grow.[16]

But wait! Let's look at how the author pictures the second kid, the mean one. Scowling, bitter, he's named "Crispin Crosspatch." Note the incredible resemblance of this name to the meaningful phrase, Christ on the Cross: *Cris*pin *Cross*patch.[17]

Crispin Crosspatch, the book reports, "is sowing lots of cross, hurtful, selfish seeds." He's depicted, too, as continually complaining and spouting nasty, negative remarks such as "woe is me," "I want more," "give me what I want," and "I hate you." "Draw the ugly, prickly plants into which they will grow," the child is instructed.[18]

Harry, who lives in the "heaven" created by his own mind, is depicted as a tender-hearted, positive, happy, loving child who helps mommy when she is tired, reminds sad kids to be brave and assists injured animals. On the other hand, Crispin Crosspath lives in the "hell" he has created for himself through his own cruel, unkind, negative thoughts and actions. Crispin Crosspath ("Christ on the Cross") suggests you trip someone up so you can win the race. He encourages you to start a fight and tempts you not to share your sweets. He's always badgering you to do something naughty. Crispin Crosspatch is one vile kid!

Later in Volume 3, children are introduced to a jigsaw puzzle of "Puppet Paul," the pieces of which they are urged to cut out and piece together. Clearly this is the *Apostle Paul* being scornfully and vilely portrayed--though silently and craftily--as a mere ragdoll, plaid-clothed puppet of Jesus. The two eyes of "Puppet Paul" are slit into *crosses* while the rest of his face resembles that of a clown.

Volume 4, GREAT TEACHERS

Children discover the fascinating life stories of the "Great" religious teachers, such as Buddha, Krishna, Muhammed, Jesus, and Moses in Volume 4. But Jesus is given no more stature and respect than any other "Great Teacher." Even Moses is His equal. Indeed, in this book produced with kids in mind, we fully discern the universal teaching of the New Age concerning Jesus. In the New Age religion, Jesus is just another man-god, another Spirit Guide, another reincarnated Master or World Teacher. He is viewed as a man who was Christ for only the time when He temporarily had the "Christ Spirit" inside Him as His guide. He is said to be *a* god or *a* Son of God, but He is *never* regarded as *the* God or *the* Son of God. Thus, in Volume 4, Jenny Dent tells kids:

> Jesus of Nazareth prepared for many lives for his incarnation as a world teacher, when he was able to bring a very special blessing to the world, and the Christ Spirit, the Son of God shone brightly through him.
>
> After Jesus' death, his followers started to insist that only he was the Son of God and that people could *only* be saved by believing in him. White Eagle (my Teacher) has given a slightly different interpretation: that people are saved by the Christ, the Son of God, the light within *them*. . . . Jesus himself did not mean for people to worship him. . . .[19]

"Jesus Did Not Really Die On the Cross"

Dent's spiritual teaching guide directs parents to tell kids that although Jesus was crucified on the cross, "he did not really die." Also, children learn that Jesus never really battled with the devil: in fact, there is no devil. The term "devil" just symbolizes the other half (the lower self) of all people:

> Jesus was tempted in the wilderness by the Devil. The wilderness symbolizes the material world and the Devil symbolizes our lower, selfish side.[20]

Buddha and Krishna Favored Over Jesus

Buddha and the Hindu God, Krishna, seem to get much more favorable treatment than Jesus. One of Dent's books includes a "Play the Buddha's Stepping Stones Game" in which kids can play some music and dance round as they learn all about Buddha's "Noble Truths."[21]

The Hindu god, Krishna, is delightfully pictured as a youth "always smiling and happy and full of joy and laughter."[22] "The teachings of Krishna," it is explained, "are contained in a book called the *Bhagvad Gita,* an important book in the world's literature, like the Bible." In the *Bhagvad Gita*, says author Jenny Dent, "Krishna is always shown dancing and playing the flute, as he brings joy and happiness into our hearts."[23]

To emphasize to the child the happy, loving attitude of the supreme Hindu deity Krishna--shown by the author to be so much more likeable and pleasant than Jesus and so much more desirable than the serious, unsmiling, solemn Jesus--the book includes an actual "Krishna Happy Mask." Kids are to color and decorate, then cut out and wear this mask, fastening it to their face and head with string or elastic. The instructions read:

> Krishna dances and plays his flute to make us happy. . . . Here's a happy mask to make. It will remind you to smile and let your light shine.[24]

New Age Visualization: The Jewel in the Lotus

Then, to further emphasize the implied superiority of Krishna over Jesus, the Christian's "Great Teacher," there is a section for the kids on New Age visualization. They are to sit quietly, picturing an open lotus flower floating on a clear pool, glistening in the light of the sun.[25] In its center, they are told, is a shining jewel. Next, the child is to:

> Concentrate on the jewel as you breathe in and out in slow gentle rhythm. Try to feel that with every in breath you are being drawn closer and closer to the jewel, the heart of the lotus, and becoming more and more in harmony with God's will . . .[26]

An Image of Ritual Sexual Intercourse

However, what neither the child nor the parent is told is what the "jewel in the lotus" symbolizes in Hindu mythology. Far from a peaceful, placid scene, the child has unknowingly been introduced to the very core, the utter essence of the Hindu religion through symbology and visualization. *The innocent child has just taken into the mind an image of ritual sexual intercourse!*

Hinduism is a religion that worships sex and the sexual union of male and female. In huge, teeming Calcutta, India each year a wild and raucous, bizarre sex festival is held in honor of Kali, the Hindu Mother Goddess. Indian men parade up and down the streets of Calcutta past cheering, demonstrative throngs of people and onlookers, holding up for everyone to see paper mache' and other replicas of the male and female sex organs.

Meanwhile, tourists and local people alike buy and cherish thousands of fetishes--small figurines, pictures, and other perversely shaped objects--of the male penis and female vagina. Musical extravaganzas also are in vogue in the streets and in homes and meeting halls and temples, with some musicians stroking the stringed instrument known as the male sitar and others playing the female sitar. As their "gender" would suggest, these musical instruments are shaped appropriately.

As did the mystery religions of the ancient Babylonians, Greeks and Romans, the Hindus teach the occult doctrine that human divinity can be attained through sexual ecstasy. Thus the literal meaning of *yoga*--the same yoga often taught in public schools to our kids as physical exercise--is "to be yoked with the gods." There is, in fact, in the Hindu religion a yoga known as *Tantra* which teaches union, or unity with the godhead through the sex act.

So in effect, the *Spiritual Teaching Series for Children* is secretly but powerfully introducing its young learners to the sick Hindu methods of attaining divinity through either mental powers (visualization) or sex, or preferably both, since many New Agers engage in sex while visualizing the "diamond" (representing the male penis) in the lotus (the female vagina).

The Dangers of Polluted Imagery

At an early age children begin to symbolize and give concrete meanings to abstract symbols and concrete objects. We all know how often, as parents and adults, we teach a child through metaphors, parables, fantasy allegories, and other word-pictures. For example, the child may hear someone call a humanitarian an "angel in disguise," may be led to believe that "fairy tales can come true," or that "storks deliver babies." This has staggering effects on the child's thought processes.

New Age teachers make maximum use of this capacity of children to develop (or stagnate) mentally and spiritually through word pictures. This is why visualization and mind-imagery is so often used on kids. It is also why the pornography and vulgarism kids see displayed so outrageously on TV, in magazines, in movies, and elsewhere is indelibly imprinted in the child's mind and later becomes so difficult to eradicate.

The Third Eye: Why Kids are Targeted

The early training of kids through projects such as the *Spiritual Teachings for Children Series* has high priority in the New Age Plan.

It is imperative, New Age and Hindu teachers alike believe, that children be introduced to New Age concepts and religious theories at a very early age. One major reason is their common belief in an invisible *Third Eye* centered in the forehead above the two physical eyes. This is related to the All-Seeing Eye of the Egyptian Sun God. When this Third Eye is "opened," assert New Age theorists, the person becomes enlightened, awake, godlike. The opening of the Third Eye is considered the pathway to immortality, human divinity, and self-empowerment.

New Agers further believe that if a person is not started early in youth to develop the opening of his or her Third Eye, it will become atrophied--closed and dead. This is what happens, they claim, when Christian fundamentalists "infect" children with their "hateful" separatist and exclusivist "Jesus-only" Bible teachings. It is therefore necessary, says Alice Bailey's spirit guide, Djwal Khul, "that opportunities be created to train the child from its earliest breath."[27]

In reality, the New Age goal is to erase the child's opportunity to come to know the real Jesus. The Master of the New Age has known for many eons that if you wish to capture and destroy an entire generation or just one child, *first, you destroy their faith in Jesus.*

FIVE

The Ultimate New Age Secret: They Plan to Take Your Children From You

Train up a child in the way he should go, and when he is old, he will not depart from it. (Proverbs 22:6)

The key answer, believe it or not, is the children. . . . If we take one generation of children and keep them enlightened, in three generations the whole world will be spiritually awakened. . . . But we have to start with one generation of children. And . . . raise them that way. (Dr. Frank Alper, *Gabriel's Horn Magazine*)

The bold New Age claim has gone out: Christian parents are ignorant, unsuitable, anti-social. They teach kids to fear the hateful Jehovah and induce in kids an Armageddon, war-like mentality. Moreover, the claim goes, Christian parents are so terrible that they actually teach their children to believe that Jesus is the *only* way and that *only their Bible* is to be believed in. All this, New Age leaders contend, is bona fide proof of separatism, disharmony, and religious bigotry. If necessary, kids should be removed from the homes of

Christians. *Christians are unfit parents, and Christian families are dangerous threats to the welfare of children.*

God Himself ordained the Christian family unit. So it is no accident that the New Age has targeted Christian families for destruction. Only in this way can kids be "liberated" from Christianity and be initiated into the New Age world religion. Only in this way can the needs of a changing planet be met. As Alice Bailey explains it, *if the New Age is to succeed, children must be provided a new environment.* The traditional family structure must be abolished so that "sensitive" children will no longer be raised by "rigid, insensitive" Christian parents:

> It is said that prior to all new growth . . . there is ever a breaking down of the old structure. Institutions and belief systems that have been formulated throughout the centuries are . . . no longer adequate to meet the needs of a changing planet.
>
> Such conditions lead us to the present problem and the resultant opportunity--an opportunity to provide . . . children with the environment which their sensitivity demands.[1]

Are Christian Parents Endangering the Spiritual Health of Children?

Satan's aim is to brand Christians as unloving, ignorant and selfish and--most of all--a threat to world religious unity. Such spiritually inferior imbeciles cannot be allowed, say New Age leaders, to raise up kids who become damaged clones and carbon copies of their parents. We must, they insist, save the kids from all this pain and suffering.

> Today the child is, for the first five or six years, the victim of his parents' ignorance and selfishness. . . . The damage done to children . . . is often irremediable

and is responsible for much of the pain and suffering in later life.[2]

Yes, say the New Age elite, our kids are being made into "sick misfits" by fundamentalist, Bible-believing Christian parents who, as everyone knows, are terrible people. "The fundamentalist Christians," snarled one New Age guru, "are the worst Christians. They are the most fanatical people. They believe that Christianity is the only religion. . . . These are primitive ideas."[3]

If you want to know just what the New Age religionists really believe and teach about Biblical Christians, all you have to do is refer to the writings of Catholic Priest Matthew Fox, currently the most raved about and admired "theologian" in the New Age. In his newest bestselling book, Fox goes to great lengths to turn people away from the Jesus of the Bible and toward the "Cosmic Christ" and the "Mother" religion.[4] He has nothing but venom for fundamentalist Christians who cleave to the Jesus who died on the cross for the sins of the world:

> Fundamentalism is the result of a deep-seated fear triggered by the break-up of social patterns. . . . Fundamentalism is patriarchy gone berserk. . . . It results from mysticism repressed and denied, and it always leads to scapegoating--the projected hatred of others.
> An almost fashionable fascism arises wherever religion or society repress the Mother principle. . . . The (fundamentalist Christian) is essentially sado-masochistic (and is) . . . the basis of a collective fascism. . . . Fascism is the ultimate expression of father dominance. . . . I call this the original sin mentality.[5]

Christians are Evil Because They Oppose World Unity

New Age theologians and teachers make clear that the problem with Christianity is its *exclusiveness*. People who accept Jesus Christ as Lord and Savior--the *real Jesus* of the Bible--and believe this is the only way to salvation, are proclaimed to be divisive. In a world where vast populations ascribe to Hindu, Buddhist, Shinto, and mystical (non-Biblical) "Christian" religions and cults, the Christian faith stands out like a sore thumb. The world cannot achieve unity until the pesky, separatist Christians are done away with. Certainly their kids cannot be trained up as Christians.

Lola Davis hits hard on the theme of world unity of all religions in her interesting but unholy book, *Toward a World Religion for the New Age*. What "we now need," she writes, is "a world religion that will teach us a world value system and some common one world goals."[6] Biblical Christianity, she makes crystal clear, simply won't do, though she lauds and compliments at least one group--the protestant World Council of Churches--for their fine progress toward world unity.

What is the answer to this terrible problem of terrible Christian parents raising up kids to be terrible Christians? Alice Bailey responds that child-care facilities *outside the home* are needed so that children will not become tainted by their parents. The New Age experts in these child care facilities will be responsible for the spiritual development of kids:

> The future will increasingly see the needs of children from a very young age being met outside the home . . . It seems apparent that state, national, and global agencies should be in the forefront of the movement towards providing child care facilities.[7]

All the New Age Needs is One Generation of Children

Dr. Frank Alper, a widely quoted New Age teacher and spirit channeler who heads the Arizona Metaphysical Society, when recently interviewed by a major New Age magazine, expressed total agreement with the New Age consensus that Christian families are detrimental to the spiritual growth of children. Alper sees a desperate need to bring in the New Age Kingdom on earth as soon as possible. How can this goal best be accomplished? His answer illuminates us to the ultimate New Age Plan:

> The key answer, believe it or not, is the children. . . .
> If we take one generation of children and keep them
> enlightened, in three generations the whole world will
> be spiritually awakened . . . as older generations die out.
> But we have to start with one generation of children.
> And . . . raise them that way. . . .[8]

Alper's interviewer, editor Kai King, excitedly expressed agreement. "We can do it!," she exclaimed. Answered Alper:

> We *have* to do it . . . so the children who come in (who
> are incarnated from a past life) will have parents who are
> aware and will know how to raise a spiritual child.[9]

Why are New Age men like Alper and women like King so emphatic--even fanatical--that our children must have *only* New Age parents who "know how to raise a spiritual child?" That answer lies in Satan's grandiose Lie to New Age believers that "Mother Earth" is to become the Planet of the Man-gods, a literal, restored planetary Garden of Eden. But, Satan interjects, this Utopia on earth can be realized *only* if the new generation of kids can be torn away from their Christian roots and repotted in "rich and fertile" New Age soil.

Today's youth, Satan confides, are rising gods, full of glory and promise. They will grow up to be New Age workmen who put the nail in the coffin of Biblical Christianity. The children *must* become pliant and submissive vassals of the New Age, servants of another God, despisers of Jesus, the old false God.

That Alper and king have bought this outrageous Lie of Satan and are now "true believers" becomes clear when we examine Alper's concluding remark:

> This is to become the Garden of Eden. This is what is supposed to be. Look at the children coming in here. Look at them! They are Ancient Masters coming to live. . . . I believe in (the) Divine Order for the evolution of this planet.[10]

In Community Alone Lies Salvation

New Age theorists contend that the spiritual needs of children can only be met by the *Community*, not by the parents. Community is the path to salvation, they say. Of course, the Community is antichrist and opposed to God. But that's the whole point. Satan does not want our children to learn the Truth about God. Thus Robert Muller, the elitist New Age teacher who formerly was Assistant Secretary-General of the United Nations, states that children in the New Age are to be taught a religion in which *many gods and religions are acceptable*, not just one. The concept of "my religion, right or wrong," Muller writes, "must be abandoned in the planetary age." [11]

The new concept of *Community* is crucial to the New Age Plan. You will be hearing more and more in the coming months and years about "Community." The Soviet Communists and Maoists in Red China use the term the *State*. New Agers have come up with a much more sinister and more devilish term: Community. It is, they say, the task of the Community to save and to dictate, to rule and to reign. *Individual salvation is out.* *"God" doesn't promise to save anymore.* His commitment is not to persons but only to all of humanity as a whole--to the Community. To unity. To oneness.

> We now enter a period wherein the goal of individual salvation is no longer appropriate. Our guidance calls for a *collective transformation.*[11]

Whose "guidance," we may well ask, calls for a "collective transformation?" Christians know *his* identity. In any case, New Age leaders have proclaimed that if Christian parents stand in the way of this collective transformation, they will be destroyed. *Only through Community can man be saved.*

M. Scott Peck, The Pied Piper of New Age Community

M. Scott Peck, the New Age "Christian" psychiatrist and bestselling author who traveled to India to study under the Hindu gurus and now practices mysticism and Zen Buddhism, denounces Christians who overemphasize Jesus' divinity as threats to the Community. They are heretics, he growls, to the emerging new spirituality, the giant leap forward into a global consciousness and a World Community where all religions are accepted:

> In and through Community lies the salvation of the world. Nothing is more important. . . . The human race stands at the brink of self annihilation. . . . I'm scared for my own skin. . . . I want to save your skin. I need you, and you need me, for salvation. We must come into Community with each other.[12]

The New Age Community is, in reality, the body of Satan. He is the head, his Community of believers the body. Therefore, Christian parents and families *are*, in fact, separatists. Praise God!

The wonderful truth is that we who are of Jesus can never fit in to Satan's world. We are a peculiar people, the few, a people culled out by God and chosen for His Kingdom. Satan's Community is not our home. We are pilgrims passing through, citizens of the most glorious of mansion worlds, where Jesus Himself sits on the throne. Heaven is our home . . . and our Community. And even now, as mortals in the flesh but with the Holy Spirit residing in our hearts, we are situated in heavenly places.

Beware of Satan's "Community" Strategy

Satan knows we who have already accepted Jesus as Saviour and Lord are a lost cause, but that does not prevent him from lusting after our children. In the contrived notion of Community, the Evil One has found a cunningly effective tool to attack Christian families and attempt to pry away our kids. His lie is that Biblical Christianity is harmful to the spiritual and mental health of children. His prescription is to take the kids from their negative Christian home environment and turn them over to New Age custodians in the Community at large.

In the near future, watch out for those who come disguised as the benefactors of our children. Community is on the march. Look increasingly for laws to be passed dictating early child care outside the home--child care devoid of Christian instruction. Look also for government-funded daycare facilities to be run by Satanists, homosexuals, lesbians and others who hate Christianity. Already reports coming in to our ministry provide ample evidence that around the nation, Family Services, Health and Human Services Departments are saturated with

New Agers, witchcraft-oriented feminists, and gays. The few Christian teachers left will attest that public schools are already infested with New Agers and secular humanists. They want your children and they are determined to have them.

The Ultimate Secret Revealed

The horrible truth--*the ultimate secret*--of the New Age is that children will eventually be taken away from their parents. This generation of young people is targeted as candidates to form a demonized, initiated corps of New Age leaders for the decades past the year 2000.

The anticipated end result is that this coming generation will willingly sacrifice American patriotism and nationalism and traditional family relationships and responsibilities for the empty New Age promise of global unity and peace. Children are now taught in many public schools that their parents' ways are outmoded and obsolete. Laws are now being tested that will make traditional Judeo-Christian lifestyles illegal.[13] In an article entitled "Parental Rights Are Not Negotiable," The Christian publication *Pro-Family Alert* crystallized the nature of the stark struggle now underway between pro-God families and the anti-God New Age leadership:

> Children are the nation's future. Whoever controls their minds will determine what the future will be spiritually, economically, and in all other ways. The social planners are keenly aware of this fact, and long-range plans have been underway for decades. These plans are being implemented with alarming speed!
> *The campaign being waged has two prongs*: one increases the rights of the government, and the other increases the rights of the child. Parents are caught in between, where their rights are weakened or destroyed.
> *This is clearly the plan* of those who are working ceaselessly to increase the power of the government in

the areas of schooling and child care. The plans extend even beyond our nation, to include global education, and this concept is embraced by many in our educational establishment and now taught in many public schools.[14]

The Magnetic Drawing Power of the New Age Cults

The planned breakdown and demise of the traditional family unit has been a bonanza for the leaders of New Age cults. It has sparked a huge growth in numbers of teenagers joining cult communities. In addition, thousands more who do not leave home nevertheless involve themselves in cult activities of one form or another.

Ken Wooden, author, occult and cults expert, and producer of a documentary on Satanism for TV's *20/20* news program, spoke at a ritualistic crime seminar for law enforcement authorities about the astonishing growth of the cults. He noted that, to be successful in luring new members, "the cults must destroy the family unit, their biggest obstacle." Therefore, separation of youth from their parents--either physically or emotionally and spiritually--is essential.[15]

Why are Youth Attracted to Cults?

Through the promotion by the cult of *oneness* with the group and by showering the new recruit with a false or inflated display of love by other cult members, the recruit is led to believe the lie that the group--in New Age terms, the *Community*--is his true family. This strategy fits in well with the New Age teaching that in Community alone lies salvation and hope for survival of the individual in a chaotic world.

The personal magnetism and charisma of the cult or group leader is yet another reason why youth are attracted to cults. Often rebellious against parents, the teenager may seek wisdom and authority from an outside "hero" or "heroine," someone they can look up to without all the parental trappings. The fake demonstrations of "unconditional love," combined with the possession by the cult leader of what seems to be mysterious "cosmic wisdom," becomes a powerful drawing card.

Major New Age Cults and Religions

Listed below are the major New Age cults, religions and religious communes, and organizations. This list is not inclusive of all such groups. In addition, remember that Satan consistently spawns and creates new groups.

In August, 1989 a very important book I am now researching will be published. This book, *TEXE MARRS BOOK OF NEW AGE CULTS AND RELIGIONS*, will be the first reliable, authoritative guide to the multitude of New Age cult groups. Every Christian parent, grandparent, pastor, ministry leader, and teacher needs this book to minister to the confused youth population targeted by the determined leaders of the New Age cults. For now, I have space in this book only for a name listing (below) of the major New Age cults, groups, religious communities, and organizations to avoid:

Astara	The Rosicrucians
Urantia	Unity Village
Baha'i	Society of Divine Love
I AM	Church of Today
Church of Scientology	Jehovah's Witnesses
Mormons (LDS)	Church of Wicca
Temple of Set	Covenant of the Goddess
Family of Love	Order of the Golden Dawn
Eckankar	EST
The Forum	Insight
Perelandra	Arcane School
Lucis Trust	Theosophy
Church of All Worlds	The Process Church

Tara Foundation
Rajneesh Foundation
The Way
Sufism (mystical Islam)
Lorian Association
Oaspe
Waldorf Schools
Ausar Auset Society
Arcosanti
Chinook Center
Findhorn
Kerista Village
Living Love
Mark-Age
Holy Order of MANS
The Millennium Society
Lifespring
Melchizedek Priesthood
Vedenta Society
Silva Mind Control
Zen Buddhism
Tantric Buddhism
Tibetan Buddhism
Seth International
The Greens

Divine Light Mission
The Uranarius Society
Soka Gakkai
Stelle Community
The Church of Satan
Anthroposophical Society
The Identity Movement
N. Vajradhatu
Shree Gurudev Ashram
Esalen Institute
Temple of Understanding
Koinonia
Sirius
Aetherius Society
Arica Institute
Great White Brotherhood
Mahayana Buddhism
Muktananda
Siddha Yoga
The Pacific Institute
Summit Lighthouse
The Farm
Yogi Bhajan
Swami Kriyananda
Serendipity

Unity School of Positive Chrisitianity
Unitarian-Universalist Church
CAUSA or the Unification Church (the "Moonies")
Church Universal and Triumphant
Center for Creation-Centered Spirituality
Bear Tribe Medicine Society
Sai Baba Ashram and groups
Self-Realization Fellowship
Worldwide Church of God (Armstrongism)
Ananda Cooperative Community
International Society for Krishna Consciousness
    (Hare Krishna)
Foundation for Inner Peace
Transcendental Meditation (TM)
Cathedral of St. John the Divine (New York City)

Yogaville (Satchidananda Ashram)
Dawn Horse Fellowship (Bubba Free John)
Association for Research and Enlightenment (A.R.E.)
Church of New Jerusalem (Swedenborg)
Church of Religious Science
Academy of Future Science (Keys of Enoch)
Maharishi International University
O.T.O. (Order Templis Orientis)
Foundation for Human Understanding
The Planetary Commission/Quartus Foundation
Center for Additudinal Healing
All Jungian groups
All Goddess groups
All Yahweh groups
All Unity churches
All Montessori groups
All Masonic orders
All Spiritualist churches
All Ramtha groups
All Enochian Magic groups
All Ancient Wisdom groups
All Native American Indian religious groups
All Rudolph Steiner groups
All Gurdjieff/Ouspensky groups
All Mystery Religion and Mystery School groups

This Dark Power that Would Harm a Child

Woe to the inhabitants of the earth and of the sea! for the devil is come down unto you, having great wrath, because he knoweth that he hath but a short time. (Revelation 12:12)

Lucifer is the angel of man's inner light. . . . He is an agent of God's love . . . and as we move into a New Age, each of us . . . must say, "Thank you Beloved (to Lucifer), for all these experiences. They have brought me to you.
(David Spangler, *Reflections on the Christ*)

Jesus loves the little children, the great old hymn goes. And He does. But Satan, the rebellious angel who dared to defy God Almighty, is just the opposite in attitude and actions toward our children. He hates them, reviles them, loathes them. Furious because he, with his insatiable appetite for power and majesty, is not on the eternal throne in Heaven, Satan has decided to become everything God is not. God is the unparalleled *lover* of children, so Satan has determined to become the supreme *hater* of youth. He is the dark power that would harm a child.

To understand the severity of the New Age assault on our kids and to comprehend what we must do to thwart this all-out New Age assault, we must first recognize just who is the master of the New Age hierarchy of demons and human counterparts. We must unmask the Master Deceiver--the god of the New Age, the ravager of the young.

Introducing Lucifer, the Lord of the New Age

Because of its deceitfulness, few realize that the New Age is in fact hard-core occultism and devil worship. Frequently this bestial nature is obscured by the gossamer thin coating of paint and glitter that is applied by Satan to fool the unwary. Believe me, though, the top people in charge of the New Age Plan to destroy our kids *know* whom they serve. And the world's best known Satanists also are in the know.

In one of the most revealing TV interviews Oprah Winfrey has ever conducted, Dr. Michael Aquino, head of the Church of Satan's Temple of Set and an avowed devil worshiper, matter-of-factly admitted that his religion was part of the New Age. Aquino spoke of a "God" of energy forces, a "God" who wanted man to enjoy carnal pleasures and self-indulgence. Then, echoing Shirley MacLaine and other New Age celebrities, Aquino sternly declared, "we are our own gods!"[1]

Oprah Winfrey, who herself is a believer in some New Age doctrines and reportedly is a member of Unity, a New Age Church, quickly responded:

> Well, the way you explain this is very much the way a lot of people who are into metaphysics now and the New Age movement and New Age thinking, they say the very same thing. Are you saying that it's the same?[2]

Dr. Aquino made it clear that, indeed, his Satanic religion and the New Age religion were bed partners: "Yes, said Aquino without hesitation, "except that I would say we Satanists have a more precise grasp of . . . this quality of the human psyche or the human soul. . . . We would say that we understand what's actually happening a little better than many New Agers."[3]

Are New Agers Satan Worshipers?

Anton LaVey, head of the worldwide Church of Satan, headquartered in San Francisco, would certainly agree with Aquino. LaVey is credited by his official biographer as "the leading causative factor in youngsters turning away from God." It is also boasted that LaVey's *The Satanic Bible* outsells the Christian Bible on college campuses."[4] Actually, this is no idle boast. My own reliable sources reveal that *The Satanic Bible*, sold in secular bookstores across America, outsells the Holy Bible almost ten-to-one in bookstores near college campuses!

LaVey, often called the "Black Pope," introduced the late actress Jayne Mansfield and a score of other famous entertainers and celebrities to the fiery world of Satan worship. He sneeringly suggests that New Age teachers are either closet Satanists who simply don't have the guts to disclose their true belief or else they are mixed up people who *think* they are worshiping themselves as "God" when in reality, they are serving their true master, Lucifer.

According to LaVey, other New Agers are just clouding the issue. They should openly admit their Satanic beliefs and quit play-acting. Instead of protesting that their "white" witchcraft and magic is "used only for altruistic purposes," for good, LaVey encourages New Age believers to confess to their involvement in a Satanic faith based on selfishness.[5]

New Agers, whom LaVey notes prefer to call themselves white "witches," *are* deceiving themselves. In his *Satanic Bible*, LaVey writes:

> White witches want to delve into witchcraft, but cannot
> divorce themselves from the stigma attached to it.
> Therefore they call themselves white magicians. . . .
> Anyone who pretends to be interested in magic or the
> occult for reasons other than gaining personal power is
> the worst kind of hypocrite.[6]

"White magic," adds LaVey, "is supposedly utilized
only for good or unselfish purposes, and black magic, we
are told, is used only for selfish or evil reasons. Satanism
draws no such dividing line. Magic is magic."[7]

Like all New Agers, LaVey does not believe in a literal Satan, but professes belief in a *God of Forces*--a
"force of nature." And also like all New Agers, LaVey
insists that man is his own god: "Every man is a god if he
chooses to recognize himself as one."[8]

The Desire for Financial Gain

We see also that the wicked Anton LaVey, founder of
one of Satan's most visible churches, heartily ascribes to
the New Age goal--also prominent among prosperity
teachers in some "Christian" churches--of striving for
financial gain, worldly power and material success. "I
break away from all conventions that do not lead to my
earthly success and happiness," LaVey trumpets. He
adds this note:

> The chief duty of every New Age is to upraise new men to
> determine its liberties, to lead it towards material
> success. . . .[9]

"No Judgment. No Hell:" The New Age-Satanist Refrain

Finally, both Aquino and LaVey make it clear that they
are in total agreement with the New Age doctrine that

denies God's judgment and an everlasting hell for sinners who reject His love. "There is no heaven of glory bright," LaVey declares, "and no hell where sinners roast." Instead, subscribing to the New Age teaching that we are our own savior, our own resurrection, LaVey stridently and blasphemously encourages all men to deny the very God, Jesus Christ, who died for their sins. "Say unto thine heart, I am mine own redeemer."[10]

This image of Baphomet, the horned goat, is frequently used in Satanic rituals.

Presenting . . . For Your Temporal Pleasure—The Prince of Darkness!

For many disciples and lower level students in the New Age, to tie their religion and beliefs with hard-core Satanism may at first glance seem extreme. After all, they have been taught that the New Age stands for universal harmony, peace, and love. How could something that sounds so good be so horribly bad?

Perhaps the most amazing aspect of the tremendous tidal wave of New Age occultism is that most of the people who are part of the New Age are so deluded they do not recognize Satan even when he comes as he is, unvarnished, as the Prince of Darkness. However, New Age teacher after New Age teacher has made plain in their teaching that Lucifer is the New Age master and that occultism is at the very foundation of the New Age.

David Spangler, former director of Scotland's Findhorn Foundation and today one of the most prominent of New Age "theologians," even calls Lucifer "the light" of this world."

> The light that reveals to us the path to Christ comes from Lucifer. . . . Christ is the same force as Lucifer.[11]

If this isn't crystal clear enough, Spangler goes on to shockingly announce that Lucifer is the "great initiator who comes to give us the final . . . Luciferic "Initiation." It is this Luciferic Initiation, Spangler assures his followers, that "is an invitation into the New Age."[12]

Not content simply to exalt Lucifer as Lord, Spangler has also called Jesus' death on the cross an "*occult* crucifixion."[13] This abominable statement is similar to a lie of New Age writer and "prophet" Benjamin Creme, forerunner of the false New Age "Christ," Lord Maitreya. Defying the Bible's clear teachings, Creme claims that it is Lord Maitreya who resurrected the body of Jesus as He lay in His tomb. "Resurrection is a very special thing technically," says Creme, "it is a great *occult* happening.[14]

In Praise of the Occult

David Spangler and Benjamin Creme are joined by a host of other New Age teachers in praising the occult and in holding up Lucifer as the real "god" or "Messiah" of the New Age. The late Alice Bailey, founder of the Lucis

Trust, originally named her group Lucifer Publishing. Helena Blavatsky, founder of the powerful international New Age occult religion and propaganda cult known as Theosophy, published a magazine called *Lucifer*.[15]

The late Edgar Cayce, author of a number of writings devoured by today's New Agers, was yet another who professed Lucifer as an angel of light. The Association for Research & Enlightenment (A.R.E.), which today perpetuates Cayce's writings, laughs at Christians who identify Lucifer as evil. Lucifer, the A.R.E. proclaims, is the "light-bringer" and the "morning star." "If we have Lucifer in our souls," the A.R.E. teaches, "we have God within."[16]

Dane Rudhyar, whose book, *Occult Preparations for the New Age*, is a bestseller in New Age bookstores, stresses that man must link up with "fallen angels"--the Occult Brotherhood of spirits in the unseen world.[17] The New Age is an occult happening, says Rudhyar, and it should be recognized as such. According to Rudhyar, the occult preparations for the New Age will succeed in bringing about the goals of "the One World of a truly organized, global community." Thus man will see the dawning of the "Millennium, a New Age global world," and a combining of two forces, which Rudhyar calls, "Sanat" and "Satan."[18]

Satan as Sanat

Rudhyar admits that the one whom many New Agers call "Sanat" is simply the flip side of the one known by man throughout history as Satan.[19] However, other New Age leaders lack Rudhyar's openness. While they enjoy boasting that their way-shower, their Lord, is Sanat, few will openly confess that Sanat is in fact Satan. This would give away the store, they believe.

Thus, Vera Stanley Alder, a well-known New Age occultist, writes that Sanat, "The Initiator," is the "Lord of the World" who comes to earth from a far off planet.[20] But then, as if she forgot what she had written, elsewhere in the same book, *The Initiation of the World*, Alder heaps praise on Satan! She declares that it is he, Satan, who is the primary ray of deity. He is the one, she exults, who oversees the New Age process of man's living many lives through reincarnation and karma.[21]

The Lucis Trust's Alice Bailey, inspired by the demon spirit who came to her as Djwhal Khul, the Tibetan Master, also has hinted at the true identity of the one whom the New Age calls "Sanat." "The name Sanat," she remarks, "is not His true name." The first two letters "Sa" are correct, Bailey confesses, "but the rest of his name remains unknown as yet" to his followers on earth. "It *is* known, however, to the Masters in the spirit world," she quickly adds.[22]

Lucifer, the New Age "God" of This World

Yes, in this instance we can certainly believe Alice Bailey when she assures us that the *real name* of this Sanat, whom she, Aquino, LaVey, Rudhyar, Creme and other New Age leaders exalt as Lord of this World, is known to those in the spirit world. He is none other than Lucifer, or Satan, for the Bible itself identifies Lucifer as the "god of this world" (II Cor. 4:4). Furthermore, we know that Satan shall remain god of planet earth, limited in his works only by the person of God the Father, until Jesus returns again in glory (Rev. 19).

Even some of the spirit channelers have brought the revelation that it is Satan, as Lucifer, who is Lord of the New Age and architect of the New Age Plan. The popular Ramtha, supposedly a 35,000-year-old, much reincarnated spirit who speaks through the lips of Seattle's spirit channeler, J. Z. Knight, has frankly stated, "In the seed of Lucifer lies God and divineness."[23]

Jose Arguelles, the New Age professor who organized the incredibly successful Harmonic Convergence gala event of August 16-17, 1987 in which hundreds of thousands of New Age faithful participated around the globe, also is a closet worshiper of Lucifer, whom he would prefer to call "Pan."[24] Arguelles' organization, the Planetary Art Network (PAN) was the group which spearheaded the Harmonic Convergence.

In Greek mythology, Pan was the god of nature. The New Age catalog *Occult Digest* (International Imports) states: "Pan is equated with Satan and life's baser aspect." Pan is known in mythology as the "horned god." Pan is also one of the exalted names attributed to Satan in Anton LaVey's *Satanic Bible*.

Edouard Schure, New Age writer and occult astrologer, reveals in his Harper & Row book, *From Sphinx to Christ: An Occult History*, the bizarre and twisted New Age belief that "the Luciferian principle, individuality and power, leads . . . to love through knowledge."[25] Schure further believes, as do most all other top ranking New Age elitists, that Lucifer is the loving hero of mankind. He is the ultimate example for man to admire and emulate:

> Lucifer, as representative of the flower of ascending humanity, corresponds to the Cult of Heroes, the greatest of whom will have their temples in the religions of the future. . . . [26]

> Even so shall the human soul, to which Lucifer gave the unassuagable thirst of the "self, the growing individuality, be filled, drop by drop, with . . . Divine Love. . . . [27]

The Gospel According to Fox: "Evil, Too, Praises God"

The Satanic spirit is painfully evident in the doctrines espoused by New Age leaders even when they do not reveal whom their true "god and hero" is. Read, for example, what the truly sinister and unrepentant pro-witchcraft Catholic priest Matthew Fox has to say about the nature of evil and about the positive aspects of darkness:

> Meister Eckhart . . . says that "All things praise God and bless God. Evil too praises God.". . . Tragic evil, though, is redemptive. It is redeemed by beauty, one might say. But to achieve its power, evil itself must become part of our dialectical way of living.[28]

> God is "superessential darkness" and to make contact with the darkness is to make contact with the deepest side of the Godhood.[29]

It can well be expected that anyone who professes a belief that "evil, too praises God" and that "God is super-essential darkness" will also have a warped, Luciferian view of who Jesus is as well. Thus, we are not surprised to discover that, like the Jehovah Witness cult, Matthew Fox does not believe that Jesus is *the* Son of God, but only *a* son of God: "Jesus is truly *a* son of God," says Fox on page 300 of his best-selling, demonically inspired Antichrist book, *Original Blessing.*[30]

As Fox's statement attests, Jesus is, to New Agers, only *a* god. Of course, in the New Age view, we are all *a* god, so Jesus is not anyone special. He's simply an animal human who worked his way through successive reincarnations to become, today, *a* god like all of us. But, to New Agers, the devil is an extra special being. Even as New Age teachers attempt to convince the world that he really doesn't exist, they teach one another that he *does exist*, as a *shadow* of each person, a *mask*, which we must come to know, appreciate, love, and heartily embrace:

> The shadow . . . the beast, the devil. . . . The devil is the multifarious figure whose features can be detected somewhere behind the persona-mask of every man and woman. It is the beast that haunts every beauty, the monster that awaits the hero on his quest. But if we recognize, acknowledge, and come to terms with it, a great deal of knowledge formerly hidden, unconscious, in the shadows, becomes conscious.
>
> When we recognize this devil as an aspect of ourselves, then the *shadow* functions as a teacher and initiator . . . providing us our greatest gift of all: self-understanding.[31]

The Devil Made Me Do It!

The New Age takes particular pleasure in ridiculing the Christian belief that the devil can and does influence men and women to commit wicked deeds and acts. Indeed, the double-minded New Age believer denies the very existence of a real devil, while at the same time he confesses to his admiration and even open worship of Lucifer. By both denying Satan and embracing Satan as Lucifer, the New Ager seeks the best of both worlds. He or she can live like the devil but claim to be a virtuous New Age god.

However, one cannot deny the evil that New Agers do *and* the evil that they are encouraging our children to do. Almost every popular ritual and practice indulged in and advocated today by New Agers was originally the invention of the devil. And it is for this reason that God's Word, the Bible, expressly forbids these practices.

The Evil New Age Influences on Our Youth

Listed below are just a few of the more prevalent New Age occult practices currently infecting the youth population, along with the corresponding passages in the Bible which clearly mark such practices as Satanically evil and forbidden:

Sorcery, Shamanism, Magic, Wizardry, Enchantments, Charms. Sorcerers, shamans, magicians, wizards, enchanters, charmers, Hindu's gurus and American Indian medicine men supernaturally wield occult and ESP powers given them by demonic spirits. These dark powers cannot be wielded until the demon spirits are conjured up through visualization and imagery or otherwise summoned. Then these agents of evil influence and bring under hypnotic and psychic control those susceptible. They use their voice and music, work with talismans, magic charms, and idols. Sometimes they cast or put a spell upon someone. Occasionally they heal through magic. Today, these Satanic agents of the New Age often prefer to be called holistic healers, psychics, humanistic or transpersonal psychologists, etc. (*Forbidden by* Lev. 19:26, Ex. 22:18, Deut. 18:10-12, II Chron. 33:6, II Kings 17:17, I Sam. 15:23, Isaiah 19:3, Isaiah 47:8-11, Jer. 27:8, 9, Dan. 1:20, Rev. 21:8, Gal. 5:19-21.)

Witchcraft. Witches are usually females, though occasionally they may be male. (Male witches are occasionally, though rarely, called "warlocks" and "wizards." These are more often literary and "show" names.) Witches practice many of the same techniques and rituals as sorcerers, shamans, and magicians. But their specialty is so-called "Earth Magic." They worship nature and the goddess, dole out herbal cures and potions and sometimes engage in ritual lesbian or other sex acts. The use of crystals is becoming more prominent among witches as are Native American Indian rituals. Many witches are radical feminists and lesbians. An amazing number of witches were formerly Catholic nuns. Some are *currently* Catholic nuns.[32] (*Forbidden by* Deut. 18:10-12, II Chron. 33:6; I Sam. 15:23, Isaiah 19:3, Gal. 5:19-21.)

Clairvoyance, Oracular magic, Soothsaying, Fortune Telling, Divination, Prognostication. Clairvoyants and similar human agents of Satan foretell events and prophesy without benefit of the Holy Spirit. Their prophesies and prognostications are actually messages they receive either from demon spirits or from their own vain imaginations. Sometimes these prophesies do not come to pass--a sure sign of a false prophet (see Deut. 18:20-22). (*Forbidden by* Jer. 27:9,10, Deut. 18:10-14, II Kings 17:17, Josh. 13:22, Micah 5:12-15, Isaiah 47:12-15, and Acts 16:16-24.)

Spirit Channeling, Necromancy, Mediumism, Spiritualism, Astral Travel. Communication with the "dead," with spirits unseen or seen, with "presences" or forces, whether they claim to be from other planets, other dimensions, other astral worlds, or other realms. An exception would be visitations by genuine angels from heaven, though such visitations--judging by the scriptures--are extremely rare. In any case, angels will always testify of Jesus and God. Also, they will uphold God's Word in our Bible. "Try (test) the spirits," John warned us in I John 4:1.

Spirit channelers allow invisible spirits to speak through their mouths. Mediums and spiritualists conjure up the spirits. The summoned spirits then either speak only to the individual, who passes on the message, or they speak to all those present. The Ouija board and crystals are also examples of demon communication, as is so-called psychic surgery. These practices are all rampant in the New Age. (*Forbidden by* Deut. 18:10-14, I Sam. 28:1-25, Isaiah 8:19, I Chron. 10:13-14, Micah 5:12-15, Acts 16:16-18.)

Astrology, Star Gazing. The analysis and divining of the supposed influence of stars, star constellations, and planetary bodies upon human behavior and events. In the Bible this was also called "observing times." It is opposed to sound Biblical doctrine because it is *God's will*, not the stars, which influences our behavior. The Bible plainly teaches that the heavens *declare* the glory of God. It does not teach, as does the New Age, that they *are* God, or that they *foretell* the future or *cause* human behavior.

New Age astrology involves not only the simple reading of horoscopes, but also the admiration and worship of the mythological gods, goddesses, and creatures of the zodiac and of the ancient pagan mythologies. (*Forbidden by* Lev. 19:26, Deut. 18:10-14, II Kings 21:6, II Chron. 33;6, Isaiah 47:12-15, Jer. 10:2, Dan. 1:18-20; 2:1-49; 4:1-37;5:7-15.)

And Much, Much More New Age Occultism

The above are only a few of the forbidden New Age occult practices being spread among our young people today. There are many others equally evil, damnable, and dangerous. These include palmistry, levitation, telepathy, tarot cards, occult numerology, hypnosis (even if induced in a psychologist's office), ecstatic dancing, fantasy role-playing games such as Dungeons & Dragons, firewalking, Satanic symbols, Egyptian magic, pendulums, UFO's, yoga, candle ceremonies and rituals, the I Ching, pagan myths (such as Taliesin, Merlin, King Arthur, Stonehenge, Atlantis, and so on), Mary worship, Druidism, and the propagation of false gospels (such as the *Forgotten Books of the Bible, The Keys of Enoch,* and so forth).

Satan surely knows that his time is short. The day is near when he will be deprived of his kingdom here on earth and he will be cast into the bottomless pit. Furiously, this wicked angelic beast is determined to lash out with all his might during the brief time he has remaining.

All of Satan's eons of trickery and deception are being poured out on this generation. The forces of good and evil are moving toward a crescendo. The ages-old struggle is nearing a grand climax and Satan is out to take as many young people with him to the pit as possible. Furthermore, since he does not know the exact time when Jesus will bring everything to a finale, Satan is in hopes that he can, by capturing this entire generation of youth, preside over a planet of pure devil worshipers by the year 2000. Satan's reasoning is like that of Nazi dictator Adolph Hitler. In the last days of his Third Reich, as his dreams of an empire crumbled, Hitler sullenly declared to his closest associates, "If I must fall, I will take as many with me as I can."[33]

SEVEN

The Unholy Childhood of the New Age Child Abusers

If thy children will keep my covenant and my testimony that I shall teach them, their children shall also sit upon thy throne forevermore.
(Psalm 132:12)

Give me your children, and I will give them the heavens, happiness, the earth, and immortality.
(Robert Muller, New Age organizer, *The New Genesis*)

On Saturday night I would see men lusting after half naked girls dancing at the carnival, and on Sunday morning . . . I would see these same men sitting in the pews with their wives and children. . . . I knew then . . . that man's carnal spirit will out!
(Anton LaVey, High Priest, Church of Satan)

Brutally and without a sign of remorse, he tortured, strangled and murdered up to 100 young girls and women. He was what is known as a serial killer. Handsome, intelligent, arrogant. How did Ted Bundy get started on the horrible road to becoming one of America's most celebrated--and repugnant--mass killers?

As my wife, Wanda, and I watched Bundy being interviewed on television by psychologist James Dobson, we saw unfold to us and the world the anatomy of his downfall. Violence and pornography in movies, TV and in print, explained Bundy, had stirred deep within him terrible depraved feelings of lust, bestiality and monstrous cruelty. It first began, Bundy confessed, when he was exposed to violence and pornography as a young teenager. It was to end the following morning in the death chamber of Florida's State Prison.

Frankly, we could not bear to watch but a few minutes of the interview. The painful thoughts of Bundy's helpless victims kept flooding into our minds, and tears would well up. So I reached for the TV controls and pushed the "off" button. At that moment, Wanda turned her face to me, looked directly into my eyes, and, in a strained but convicting voice, said, "Texe, that man was once some mother's baby boy."

In the days that followed, I pondered often on Wanda's insightful comment. "Texe, that man was once some mother's baby boy." The words seared my mind and conscience. *It struck me that every mass murderer, from Hitler to Stalin, from Manson to Bundy, once had been some mother's baby boy.* So, too, had every hardened and dedicated New Age occultist. What had gone wrong in their lives? As children, what sinister influences had possibly shaped their souls to cause them later to reject Jesus and go after demons, false gods, and a life of perversity?

The Anatomy of Seduction

It is important that we keep in mind that *every one of today's New Age occultists was once a child.* For example, consider such unholy New Age leaders as Anton LaVey, High Priest of the Church of Satan, and David Spangler, author and past director of the Findhorn New Age

community. How did these men come to be possessed by
the Lord of the Underworld? Did something happen to
them in childhood that set them on their current pathway
to destruction? Is there anything we can glean from
learning about their childhood that will aid us in prevent-
ing our own children from following a similar dangerous
path?

My research demonstrates that each of these men had
occultic experiences during their youth. These experiences undoubtedly shaped their later behavior. It can be
safely stated that these two New Age leaders--each of
whom deny the true Jesus Christ and His Word--were
molded as children to believe in unholy principles of the
New Age World Religion that had begun to take final
shape.

LaVey's Childhood: A Time of Vampires and Witches

Anton LaVey's story is perhaps most dramatic. In the
introduction to *The Satanic Bible*, LaVey's childhood is
explored and briefly detailed by author and confidant,
Bert Wolfe. A grandmother, Wolfe explains, evidently
passed on to Anton the legends of vampires and witches.
"As early as the age of five, LaVey was reading *Weird
Tales* magazines and books such as Mary Shelly's *Frank-
enstein* and Bram Stoker's *Dracula*.[1] Wolfe further states
that:

> In high school LaVey became something of an offbeat
> child prodigy. Reserving his most serious studies for
> outside the school, he delved into music, metaphysics,
> and secrets of the occult. Bored with high school classes,
> LaVey dropped out in his junior year, left home and
> joined the Clyde Beatty Circus.[2]

LaVey, then only 16-years-old, was assigned a number of circus tasks. One was to feed the lions and tigers. Another job he had was that of playing the organ at the carnival lot. In his own words, LaVey describes how he came to the conclusion that the Christian Church is sadly deficient and why he decided to found the Church of Satan:

> On Saturday night I would see men lusting after half-naked girls dancing at the carnival, and on Sunday morning when I was playing the organ for tent-show evangelists at the other end of the carnival lot, I would see these same men sitting in the pews with their wives and children, asking God to forgive them and purge them of carnal desires. And the next Sunday they'd be back at the carnival or some other place of indulgence.
>
> I knew then that the Christian Church thrives on hypocrisy, and that man's carnal nature will out![3]

A Motivation for Christians

This is, of course, LaVey's own lame excuse for his later debauched evil conduct. We need not necessarily accept what he says as either meaningful or even truthful. But it does indicate a certain, cynical frame of mind that Satan loves to cultivate in our teenagers. It also provides Christian men with the incentive and motivation to always conduct themselves in a holy and righteous, non-hypocritical manner. We never know when a young man much like Anton LaVey may be watching us to see if our external behavior is in keeping with our profession of faith in Jesus.

It is high time that Christian adults strive to exemplify the high standards that God has set for His elect, especially in an age when the whole world is so quick to point fingers and say, "See, look there! He (or she) claims to be a Christian!"

Moreover, can we risk allowing our children, in their early, formative years, to read and contemplate horror and occult fantasy books and magazines? And what of the violent slasher movies so many uncaring or unwise parents--even Christian parents--permit their kids to watch? LaVey's mind, at age five, was filled with the perverse thoughts and ideas acquired from his being told occultic stories about vampires and witches. Later, he avidly studied occult books and developed an intense interest in occultic music. What about *your* child?

David Spangler's Religious Calling

In his book, *Emergence*, New Age leader David Spangler reveals that while he was yet in college in California, he experienced "something akin to a religious call." It was, he relates, "an inner part of me *that had earlier said yes* to the idea of a New Age."[4]

Spangler's testimony also reveals these *earlier* circumstances from which his New Age calling stemmed. It resulted, he writes, from his experiences in youth:

> Because of my background of psychic and mystical experiences during childhood that had left me with a deep interest in the nature of spirituality and the role of the *invisible*, formative side of life, that inner call won out.[5]

Psychic and mystical experiences in his childhood years put Spangler solidly on his path to becoming, today, one of the world's foremost New Age evangelists. Childhood curiosity, but, tragically, curiosity unleavened by the Truth of Jesus Christ and the Word of God. Regrettably, spiritual curiosity devoid of direction by the Holy Spirit leads in only one direction: *downward*, toward the abode of the Evil One.

Again, there are vital, significant lessons for us in the example of David Spangler. Is your child exhibiting a keen interest in spiritual things? Is his curiosity and fascination filled up with the vivid, life-changing truths and parables, case studies and holy examples contained in God's Word? Or, is your child forced to develop his or her own brand of spirituality by default?

Children are Hungry for Truths

Anyone who is around a young child for any length of time well knows of a child's inquisitive, exploratory attitude. Children love to question, to probe, to discover something exciting and new, something profound and meaningful they can embrace as Truth. The New Age child abusers prey on this inquisitive but trusting inherent capacity of the child.

Examples of this abuse abound. For example, in a recent issue of *Life Times* magazine, a young girl, Rami, age eight, was interviewed. The tale told by little Rami (the name is of Hindu origins, meaning "God, the Ram") provides proof of the brainwashing that many such children are today receiving from their New Age parents and teachers. Listen to Rami as she recounts her imaginative story of reincarnation and her "angel:"

> Before I came to earth my angel blessed me. She told me I would be having a good mother and father and sister too.
> I felt exalted and happy to come to earth. I felt a drop sad to leave my heaven friends, but I knew I could come back in my sleep to visit.
> My angel . . . said she would stay close to me and I could pray to her if I needed help.[6]

How vulnerable our kids are! We know that God does have his angels and the Bible instructs us that angels occasionally--though rarely--bring messages or instructions from God. But we pray not to them but to God and

His Son. Rami has also been set up to believe that she existed previously and was *reincarnated* into her current body. Again, this is an unholy lie and this young girl is its victim, for we are told in Hebrews 9:27 that it is appointed for a person *once* to die.

New Age author and seminar leader, Chris Griscom, gives yet another example of how children are being brainwashed. She provides an account of the time she took her three children to a *firewalking* event. In firewalking, the participants march briskly barefoot across a bed of live hot coals. It is claimed by its proponents that firewalking is a miracle and a display of mind power because the participants are not severely burned. Actually, scientists have repeatedly explained that there is no miracle involved at all in firewalking. The secret is simply to keep a brisk pace as you step across. The moisture on the sole of the feet takes care of the rest. Unaware of this scientific fact, participants in firewalking events come away from the experience convinced that a miracle has occurred.

This is Griscom's description of what happened when her 13-year-old Megan approached the hot coals:

> Megan stepped to the edge. I remember how my breath and heart became stilled. I watched her young grace as she glided across with a sureness that brought tears to my eyes. She circled around to stand next to me and in a very strong, knowing voice said, "Mom, I'll never have to die of cancer. Maybe I'll never die at all."[7]

Here we see the classic devastating result of a false miracle: unquestioning belief by a person being deceived. Because she succeeded in a sham firewalking stunt, young Megan, age 13, obviously became convinced that she would not have to someday die of a dread cancer. Indeed, she exclaimed to her approving mother, "Maybe I'll never die at all."

The Testimony of Alice Braemer

If the New Age occultists can reach a youngster early enough, that child may end up irreparably scarred for life. But we should never forget that Jesus can rescue even the most severely brainwashed child from the clutches of Satan.

One of the most fascinating and inspiring true-life accounts I have read of a person accepting Jesus as Lord and Savior is that of Alice Braemer. Alice was astrologer Jeanne Dixon's assistant for seven long years, and her testimony of that period is itself revealing. However, even prior to this, Alice was involved in New Age activities. She became enamored first with the New Age cult church called Unity. Later she got involved in the study and practice of Christian Science, another New Age cultic church.

Neither of these New Age cults believe in a literal devil, and no one had ever warned Alice about these groups being demonic. Indeed, she was taught that literal demons did not exist.

In her book *Cultism to Charisma*, Alice Braemer tells of the effect on her son, Carlton, of the New Age occultism to which he was exposed growing up as a child in her home:

> We didn't think too much about it when Carlton went out and bought his own pack of cards and purchased his own tea and tea cup. But one thing led to another and before we knew it, Carlton was going to the Library of Congress to find out about witchcraft. By that time he had also been committed to the mental hospital from which he was later released.
>
> Carlton was a terrible problem to us. We never could understand what went wrong and no one can imagine the constant fear and terror I went through year after year, because we never knew when he would become violent.

Since we were students of Christian Science, it just never occurred to us that Carlton's problem was demonic, until that fateful day when I heard him giggling in his room and invoking the name of Lucifer! That did it! Instantly, *instantly*, a veil was torn from my eyes. I could see clearly, for the first time, that Satan was alive and well on the planet Earth.

Nothing will ever be the same for us. It was the point of no return--the crisis, the crossroads--the turning point in our lives! In my despair I cried out to God, and in His mercy, He rescued us.[8]

Satan's Fate is Sealed

Today, Alice Braemer is a dedicated Christian woman with a power-packed testimony for our Savior. Praise God she has agreed to open her heart and reveal to the world those horrendous things that happened to her and her family before she came to know Jesus. *Alice now recognizes that, today, Satan may be alive and well on planet Earth, but not for long.* Jesus prophesied He would return again to put an end to the brutality and wicked deceptions of the dungeon master (Matthew 24). And He will.

In the meantime, we who love children and want the best for them cannot afford to make light of Satan's presence or to discount the impact his New Age Plan is having on our kids. As Paul instructed, we are not to be ignorant of the devices of the devil. We owe our children--and our God--more than that.

The New Age Commitment to Steal and Destroy Our Kids

If we are to successfully challenge Satan's New Age strategists, we need first to understand the depth of their commitment to steal and destroy our kids. Satan's serpentine wisdom is diabolically shrewd. He knows that he is on the very threshold of winning an entire generation of children. This is the moment for which he has lusted for centuries. He has viciously seized our children by the jugular veins and, like a junkyard dog, he won't let go until his savage work is completed . . . or until our Lord Jesus--his conqueror on the cross 2,000 years ago--returns to put him out of his misery.

The evidence that today's depraved New Age child abusers have targeted our kids--have made their destruction top priority--is massive. Marilyn Ferguson, editor of the *Brain/Mind Bulletin,* and the landslide bestseller so dear to New Agers entitled *The Aquarian Conspiracy,* complains currently that it is difficult to usher in the New Age because some in the older generation are resistant to change. "It requires such a radical shift that the people who grew up with the old framework of belief find it very hard to buy," she groans.[9]

But, like others of the New Age elite, Ferguson has the solution: go after the kids; win over the minds of the rising generation. "It may take a new generation growing up with the new idea for it to gain acceptance," she says.[10]

Will Satan Possess Our Kids by the Year 2000?

Indeed, many in the New Age propose that it will be the year 2000 or shortly thereafter perhaps before the New Age can fully become reality. Gloria Steinem, the ardent feminist admired by so many New Agers, declares, "By the year 2000 I hope we will raise our children to believe in human potential instead of God."[11]

The New Age leadership is working hard to make Steinem's target date of 2000 AD a reality. In the interim, our youth, from toddlers to teens, are primed for exploitation. Alice Bailey explains why:

> The future of the race lies in the hands of the young
> people everywhere. They are the parents of the coming
> generations and the engineers who must implement the
> new civilization. What we do with them . . . is
> momentous in its implications; our responsibility is
> great and our opportunity unique.[12]

New Age leaders are leaving nothing to chance.
While they mount a tremendous effort to capture our
teenagers, nevertheless they also have a highly concerted
campaign in motion to reach kids who are four, five and
six years of age. Even babies in the cradle are considered
candidates for New Age conquest. Djwhal Khul, Alice
Bailey's "Tibetan Master," contends that:

> The real work . . . should be started in infancy so that the
> consciousness of the child (so easily directed) can from
> its earliest days . . . be formulated.[13]

Khul ingeniously maintains that raising up the child to
conform to New Age standards from infancy, such progress can be made that, by adolescence, the youth shall
willingly devote himself in service to the New Age Plan:

> Finally the time will come, under these conditions, when
> in late adolescence . . . he will stabilize himself in the
> particular manner in which destiny ordains that he shall
> fulfill his task of right relationships through the means
> of vocational service.[14]

The Lie: Your Children Do Not Belong to You

To the New Age leadership, our children are considered
like little robots in some future robot factory, waiting
aimlessly in an assembly line for their brains to be
crammed and programmed with scads of *anti*-God, pro-
New Age information. They do *not* belong to parents.

They belong to Satan, who is reverently but hazily referred to by New Age theologists as the *Presence*, the *Collective Consciousness*, the *Higher Self*, the *Universe*, the *Universal Mind*, the *Force*, or by any one of a profusion of other equally mindless names.

For example, in his book, *How to Raise a Child of God*, New Age educator Tara Singh uses the "wisdom" found in the false bible known as *A Course in Miracles* to propound the theory that parents are not truly parents. They do not own the child but are mere "custodians." The child, Singh says, belongs to the "Universe" and must be brought up according to "Universal Laws."[15] It goes without saying that the Universal Laws set forth by Tara Singh in his books are not those found in our Holy Bible. Their source is most definitely *not* heavenly.

The Truth: Children Are an Heritage of the Lord

The facts are far different from what Tara Singh and his New Age henchmen would have you believe. Children do not belong to the "Universe" but to God the Father. They also belong to parents for children are the gift of God, and parents have a grave responsibility to raise them in admonition of the Lord. As the Bible teaches us, "Lo, children are an heritage of the Lord, and the fruit of the womb is His reward (Psalms 127:3).

We know also that children are to be taught to love God above all else and to understand His mercy and His unending supply of forgiveness. They are also to be instructed to fear God, for He alone is Holy and righteous and deserving of all honor and praise. And children should learn to value God's incomparable Word. As the Psalmist writes, "Forever, O Lord, Thy Word is settled in heaven" (Psalm 119:89).

These are the straight facts, the incontrovertible Truth, for they spring up direct from the External

Source, our Lord and God. But from the pen of Robert Muller, one of the world's best known New Age teachers and propagandists, comes these dramatic, boastful words. Read them over and consider *their* original source, for Muller himself has admitted that his guidance comes from the spirit world:

> Give me your children, and I will give them the heavens, happiness, the earth, and immortality.[16]

Satan Cannot Deliver on His Promises

It is just like Lucifer to arrogantly boast of what he cannot deliver. In the Old Testament we find Lucifer solemnly and rather pompously declaring, "I will ascend into heaven, I will exalt my throne above the stars of God" (Isaiah 14:13). Then the prophet Isaiah (chapter 14:15) delivers to Lucifer this ringing pronouncement from God: "Yet thou shalt be brought down to hell, to the sides of the pit."

Now, in these final, momentous years of the 20th Century, we once again hear Lucifer's arrogant but idle declaration, "Give me your children," he insists, "and I will give them the heavens, happiness, the earth and immortality."

Like Isaiah, our response should be immediate, bold, precise, and to the point. "No, Lucifer, you *cannot* have my child. You are a liar and the father of lies. You bring only misery and death. And God has already judged and sentenced you. The heavens are not yours to give and soon even earth shall be rid of you. Your fate is sealed by the unchangeable Word of God:

> And I saw heaven opened, and behold a white horse; and He that sat upon him was called Faithful and True, and in righteousness He doth judge and make war.
>
> (Rev. 19:11)

And He was clothed with a vesture dipped in blood: and His name is called the Word of God. (Rev. 19:13)

And He hath on His vesture and on His thigh a name written, KING OF KINGS, AND LORD OF LORDS. (Rev. 19:16)

And the devil that deceived them was cast into the lake of fire and brimstone, where the beast and the false prophet are, and they shall be tormented day and night forever and ever. (Rev. 20:10)

The Great Brain Robbery: The New Age Seduction of America's Classrooms

Hear O Israel: The Lord our God is one Lord: And thou shalt love the Lord thy God with all thine heart, and with all thy soul, and with all thy might. And these words which I command thee this day shall be in thine heart. And thou shalt teach them diligently unto thy children. . . .
(Deuteronomy 6:4-7)

Young people (in schools) will be graded into two groups: the mystical . . . and the occult.
(Alice Bailey/Djwhal Khul, *Education in the New Age*)

Seizing total control of the education of our children is a paramount goal of the New Age leadership. Incredibly powerful forces have been marshalled around the U.S.A. and the globe to concentrate on turning school classrooms into experimental New Age learning laboratories. The New Age assault extends to *every* school in America, even to day care, pre-school and kindergarten. It continues through college and university study.

The teacher training programs are also a target, because Satan's objective has been, first, to capture the souls of teachers and educators. Then, as energized New Age believers, the educators are to go forth and become "Change-Masters," boldly proselytizing and promoting the unholy New Age gods and doctrines *inside* the classroom. This process has been underway for decades but is now escalating.

Smuggling and Sneaking-in New Age Doctrines

Much of what has been actively going on in our classrooms has been kept hidden from the view of parents. The New Age conspiracy in education has done--and is still doing in many school districts--its dirty work behind closed school classroom doors.

New Age educator Virginia Essene provides these "Guidelines" for teachers to secretly teach the New Age religion in her book *New Teachings for an Awakening Humanity:*

> I urge every teacher and educator of whatever grade and subject to take the initiative in preparing a curriculum. Do not let the fear that you might be accused of putting religion into the schools hamper your usefulness in spreading the truth. There are many ways these lessons can be taught. . . . Use whatever vocabulary allows you to obey the regulations of the public schools. . . . Be creative. . . .[1]

Gay Hendricks and Russell Wills, in their book on New Age visualization, mental imagery, and meditation, explain to teachers that a number of different names could be used for this type of instruction: "Quiet time," "relaxation," and "head ed." "Or," the authors suggest, you might call the activities "centering."[2]

In other words, to get by the objections of Christian fundamentalist parents who might object, just change the names in the curriculum, say New Age educators. Smuggle and sneak it in, if necessary, *but do it!*

The Montessori Curriculum

One of the new curricula being foisted on our kids that desperately needs to be exposed is *Montessori.* Recently I spent many hours examining the documentation on this curriculum that is being implemented in classrooms across America. It's called the "Montessori Method," after its founder, the late Maria Montessori.

The Montessori curriculum is of great interest to me because many years of my life have been spent in educating young people. Holding a graduate degree in education, I have taught for three universities and supervised educators. But as I read these materials, I began to weep and cry. How could they do these horrendous things to our helpless, innocent children, I cried out from the depths of my being. How could they!

It's all there in the official Montessori curriculum: the Mother Goddess, Earth and nature worship, the occult symbols, the New Age fantasy tales of Atlantis and Lemuria, the Hindu psychology, the Nazi Aryan super race theory, the Egyptian mythologies, the Cosmic Plan, the "perfect human" lie, the Universal Oneness theme.[3]

Maria Montessori: The New Age-Nazi Connection

Who was this Maria Montessori, whose education methods and thinly veiled religious beliefs are being promoted today in over 3,000 public school districts across the U.S.A.? Even some of her staunchest supporters admit that she and Fascist Italy's Benito Mussolini worked closely together in the 1920's and 1930's to bring her teachings to bear throughout Italy. Indeed, dictator Mussolini was at one time the President of the Montessori Society of Italy![4]

Montessori's fame then spread to Nazi Germany where the Montessori Method found favor with Adolph Hitler's education overlords. Montessori was a great friend of the occultic group, Theosophy. In India, she lived and worked with Theosophy leaders, who also published a number of her works. Hindu leader Ghandi praised her work and her "method." Her system of "Cosmic Education" was especially pleasing to the Hindus and Theosophy.[5]

Today, the Montessori Method of "positive education" is taught at the New Age commune of Elizabeth Clare Prophet, head of the cultic Church Universal and Triumphant in California and Montana. Indeed, Prophet, who believes that her spirit guide, Count St. Germain, is superior to Jesus, has founded a group called Montessori International.[6] Thousands of Montessori schools have sprung up across the U.S.A. and the world, many begun by ardent New Agers and occultists, others by sincere but misguided educators.

Montessori to Bring in World Peace and "A New Type of Man"

The North American Montessori Teachers Association (NAMTA), in affiliation with the Montessori Association International (AMI), glowingly describes the influence of Maria Montessori on the new educational method being prescribed today for so many thousands of schools. This method can help to bring in *world peace*, they claim because, as Montessori herself stated, it will result in "A new type of man, a better humanity." [7] It will also, NAMTA comments, help man succeed in the

"global task" of "reconstruction."[8]   In a recent NAMTA
Journal, the educators stated:

> Maria Montessori, along with many other enlightened
> thinkers of our time, foresaw nothing less than the
> emergence of a new human culture. This new culture, a
> global, planetized humanity, would be based on a new
> consciousness of the unity and interdependence of all
> being, the interconnectedness of all forms of energy and
> matter. It is the culture of the present paradigm shift, by
> which we are beginning to align ourselves to educate the
> human potential for conscious cooperation with the
> evolution of life on the planet.[9]

The above statement parrots the typical New Age line
with all its talk about "New human culture," "global,
planetized humanity," "new consciousness," "unity,"
"interdependence of all forms," "energy," "paradigm
shift," "human potential," "conscious cooperation," and
"evolution."[10]

The North American Montessori Teachers Association (NAMTA) recognizes the New Age religious
doctrine of reincarnation--also a principal, guiding belief
of their founder, Maria Montessori. The organization
encourages teachers and educators to help the "incarnat-
ing" child find "her" own place in the cosmos. NAMTA
also calls on teachers to fulfill the "vision" of founder
Montessori:

> Our task as Montessori educators has a new dimension.
> A first goal has always been to help the child find her
> own place in the cosmos, which includes incarnating and
> being humanized by the micro-culture. In addition, we
> must aid the child to transcend the micro-culture and to
> incarnate the globalized/planetized culture without
> which we as a species will not survive.
> Our Montessori legacy is a rich one, for it contains
> both the vision and the means to implement it. At every

developmental level, from toddlerhood on, we teach the needs of people. Cosmic Education is a daily experience as children and adults from many cultural and language groups come together. Within that diversity, we offer a curriculum based on cooperation, interdependence, and respect for all forms of life. We offer a curriculum that honors individual and group differences while emphasizing our essential connectedness to each other and to the Earth. In Maria Montessori's time, hers was a futurist vision. In ours, it is the vision of *now*.[11]

Religion Returns to School . . . But What Religion?

In addition to such New Age curriculum "innovations" as the Montessori Method, there is another hurricane brewing today, involving the teaching of religion in public schools. First, the New Age Plan called for the removal of all religion--meaning *Christianity*--from the classroom. This has been done. Now comes Phase II of the New Age Plan--*put religion back into the schools. But not the Christian religion--the New Age World Religion!*

Almost every major teacher and educator group and association has recently spoken out in favor of religion being returned to classrooms. Hinduism, Buddhism, even witchcraft and pagan religions are to be taught. Christianity is to be only a small, insignificant and isolated part of this new religious curriculum.

The New Age is now able to sneer at Christian fundamentalists, and scathingly say, "Okay, you wanted religion in schools, we'll give you religion. *Our* religion. And there's nothing you can do about it!"

There *is* something Christian parents can do about this, but we are going to have to insist on our rights. Dennis L. Cuddy, Ph.D., a Christian who was formerly senior associate with the National Institute of Education and on the advisory council to the U.S. Secretary of Education, recently commented that the new trend of teaching Eastern religions in schools is a violation of church and state and is, as it is now occurring, unconstitutional. Dr. Cuddy noted that at one high school a teacher uses incense as part of his instruction about a particular religion. At a different high school, the teacher directed the students to meditate as part of the instruction about Hinduism. As Dr. Cuddy observed:

> The problem with this is that if the Supreme Court recently declared even "a moment of silent meditation" unconstitutional because it "might be" religiously related, then certainly the forementioned instruction in our public schools would be unconstitutional as well.[12]

The Vicious New Age Attack on Our Kids

The adoption of the occultic Montessori system by public schools and the teaching of Eastern religions are only two instances of the universal New Age attack on our children. Satan has left no stone unturned as he seeks to destroy our kids.

Not a day goes by that we do not get letters from parents shocked and alarmed about New Age and occult influence in their children's classroom. In Buffalo, New York, an elementary school teacher led her students through a Silva Mind Control visualization exercise so they could "actually see and talk with the long-dead spirits of George Washington, Abraham Lincoln and other famous men from the dead." In Round Rock, Texas, 4th graders of a "World Culture" class were told by their teacher to put their backs against the wall, stretch forth their arms and hands, and chant, "All hail the power of the mighty globe."

Public school teachers sympathetic to the New Age World Religion are teaching Yoga and occult meditation right in the classroom; they are forcing youngsters to use crystals in basic math to help improve memory powers, conducting seances, and even, in a few cases, carrying out a witchcraft ritual as a "learning aid." Homework assignments by some teachers include theme papers on the occult, witchcraft, suicide and Satan.

Meanwhile, school libraries are well stocked with occult books that teach kids how to be a witch, learn occultic alphabets and symbols, and exercise ESP powers.

Amazingly, today it is illegal to pray even for a moment in school classrooms. The teaching of Christianity is absolutely off limits. But there's no impediment whatsoever to instruction in Eastern religions and the occult.

Recently, Jim McClellan, host of Trinity Broadcasting Network's popular "Joy" television program, related that his youngest son had come home from school one day with a copy of the Satanic text, *The Book of Shadows*, in hand. He explained to his dad that the kids were studying witchcraft in class. Shocked, Jim called the local American Civil Liberties Union (ACLU) chapter. "Would you consider tackling a case in which religion is being taught in public schools?," Jim asked. "Yes, indeed!" was the reply. "Well," Jim said, "the case involves the religious teachings of the Church of Wicca (witchcraft), an organized religion." "Oh, we're not interested," the ACLU representative snapped. "We thought you meant that Christianity was being taught. We're very much against that."

The New Plan to Take Over Our Schools

The New Age invasion of our classrooms is not accidental. It has been planned and systematically carried out by New Age educators. Their basic plan for conquest of schools is contained in the book, *Education in the New Age*, written by Alice Bailey and first published by Lucis Trust (formerly Lucifer Publishing Company) in 1954. That's almost four decades ago!

In the foreword to *Education in the New Age*, Professor Dr. Oliver L. Reiser, Department of Philosophy at the University of Pittsburgh, writes that teachers, educators and parents must work to instill a *New Age worldview* in the minds of students. This worldview, according to Reiser, must be built on "Universal principles" extracted from all the world's religions. To properly insure such a worldview, Reiser calls for a One World Government and a Planetary Worldview.

> Accordingly we need . . . the political synthesis of a
> World Federation . . . a planetary way of life, a planetary
> ethics, and a planetary way of feeling. . . .[13]

Considering this emphasis by Reiser and Bailey and their demon guides which began some 35 years ago, it is easy to understand why, over the intervening years, educators have pushed for Global Studies, World Culture and World Religion curricula to be adopted by almost all the U.S.A.'s school districts.

Guidelines found in *Education in the New Age* also reveal to us why the mystical and the occult are now proliferating in our classrooms. For example, Bailey encourages the following procedure:

> Young people will be graded into two groups: the
> *mystical*, under which heading one would group those
> with religious, artistic, and the more impractical
> tendencies; and the *occult*, which would include the
> intellectual, scientific, and mental types. By the time a
> child is seventeen the training given should have enabled
> him to strike his note clearly and should have indicated
> the pattern into which his life impulses will probably
> run.[14]

The Goal of New Age Education: Creation of the New Man-god

The ultimate goal of New Age education is to create an entire new species of human being: *Aquarian Man.* As Djwhal Khul, through Alice Bailey, remarks, "We are laying the foundation for the emergence of a new species of human being--a more evolved unit within the human family."[15] Teachers are urged to discriminate in favor of students whose New Age family backgrounds and spiritual race level predispose them toward this evolutionary goal.

Vera Alder is even more specific in her book, *When Humanity Comes of Age.* She groups all people into spiritual races, the highest of which are *Aryan* and *Aquarian* man. An advanced Aryan, she says, has the inherent capacity or potential to become an Aquarian with the proper New Age education. The Aquarian is the race of man-gods on planet earth. This is New Age man.[16]

LEMURIAN   ATLANTEAN   ARYAN (PISCEAN)   ARYAN (AQUARIAN)

Vera Alder's depiction of the New Age spiritual race theory. The Aquarian (far right) is fair, blond and blue-eyed, just the same as Adolph Hitler's superior race.

Alice Bailey and her spirit guide, Djwhal Khul, suggest that an important task of teachers and educators is to cull or select out the kids who are Aquarians and the ones who have the potential to become Aquarians and give these specially gifted children all the attention and special treatment they deserve.

> They will be safeguarded and not punished; they will be stimulated and not held back; they will be occultly recognized. . . .
>   These children must be watched from babyhood, their parents must be willing to cooperate . . . and their lives (their case histories) must be studied.[17]

What of the Children of the Inferior "Christian" Race?

So the children of the exalted race of New Agers are to receive favored treatment in the new system of universal New Age education. What, then, is to become of the children of "less spiritually advanced" parents? What of the kids of Christians whom New Age teachers and educators decide to label as members of the Lemurian, Atlantean, or the *lower* (early) Aryan races? The shocking answer is that Christian children are to be treated as an ignorant and inferior species incapable of learning. They are to be victimized by discrimination. As Alice Bailey explains:

> The imposition of the New Age ways in education upon a child who is basically Atlantean or early Aryan in his consciousness, is a fruitless task and will really do little to help him. It is for this reason that a careful analysis of the child must be made from the very moment of birth. Then, with as full information as possible, the educator will endeavor to meet the need of the . . . major types of children.[18]

To implement the New Age racial selection process in schools will take much preparation, Bailey explained. First, she suggests that textbooks be rewritten. The idea of nationalism will be thrown out and the "global community" will find its place in school textbooks. "Separative" ideas--such as Christianity being the only true religion or the concept of patriotism to one's country--will also be discarded. The beauty of humanity will be emphasized.[19]

Educators will also work to eliminate the competitive spirit in the classroom.[19] The Montessori Method, with its permissive, noncompetitive environment, is therefore ideal.

Religion and Education to Fuse

The New Age Plan to seduce children in the classroom is already far advanced. Satan believes that education holds the key to his success in winning the entire world to his cause. As Vera Alder writes, the Plan is to *"fuse"* education and religion so perfectly that "In the future it would be impossible to say where religion, education, and daily living begin or end."[20]

NINE

Sex and Sorcery: The Incredible Comic Book Horror Show

For this purpose the Son of God was manifested, that He might destroy the works of the devil.

(1 John 3:8)

I am the master of the shadows . . . and I claim this church as my own. I smell blood, the blood of the Lamb. He's here. DRIVE HIM OUT!

(*The Gargoyle* comic book, *Marvel Comics*)

C omic books have changed. Perhaps you fondly remember the days when as a child you spent many contented hours reading the good and pure morality tales of humor, light fun and adventure then prevalent in comics. If so, you will no doubt be utterly shocked and appalled to discover how successful Satan has been in taking his message straight to this new generation in the most sneaky route possible: via comic books.

On shopping forays recently I purchased close to a hundred of today's hottest comic books. These comic books are the same ones sold from the wire racks and shelves at your local supermarket, 7-11 convenience mart, variety store, or bookstore. When I got home and began to carefully examine my purchases, my mind grew numb and my heart raced. *There in the pages of comic books--comic books no less!--was the complete teaching curriculum of the New Age and the occult.*

I could even give course titles to the various comic book series. For example, one could well be titled *Introduction to Demons and Their Subterranean Master.* Another, *All About the Goddess* and yet another could appropriately be labeled, *Why the Christian Church is Evil and Must be Replaced by the New Age World Religion.* There could also be comic book course titles such as *Sex and Kiddie Porn in the New Age* and *One Million Ways to Kill and Torture for the Pure Joy of It.*

Comic Books: The Perfect Medium for Satanic Education

I am quite sure that many parents innocently buy their children these comic books without any idea of how atrocious and demonic are the contents. After all, what harm could there be in a mere comic book, right?

Again, we have to understand what we are dealing with here. The New Age Plan calls for New Age occultic ideas to be imparted to kids *by all available means.* What better way, then, to secretly infect the minds and souls of youth than through comic books?

Comic books provide three prime advantages to Satan. First, they combine the written word with vivid and colorful pictures and imagery. Thus, the ideas conveyed and acts and behavior portrayed on the pages of comic books can have a doubly powerful, long-lasting effect and impact.

Second, comic books are a cheap and efficient way to get out the New Age message. These tools of Satan cost the buyer only about 75 cents to a dollar. So they sell in the millions.

Third, while parents may look suspiciously on TV and movies, most do not suspect comic books as harboring evil and darkness. Consequently, the New Age sees comic books as a bright field in which to recruit our children for Satan's last days army.

Fingering the Christian Church as Monstrously Evil

A number of comic books have viciously anti-Christian themes and plots. Others offer up all the religious doctrines and practices of the New Age such as reincarnation, spirit channeling, crystals, and psychic powers, while implying that these are normal and respected by society. The child is led to believe that it is perfectly okay to practice occult methods and to call up demons and spirits, etc. He or she also is led to believe that Christian fundamentalists who oppose such practices are weird fun-stoppers at best, evil monsters at worst.

New Age Heroes to the Rescue!

An example of a comic book series that goes all-out to poison our children's minds against true, Biblical Christianity, is *The Gargoyle*. In this 24-page volume and its sequels is a summary of everything the New Age would like to get across to our youth. This comic book paints the New Agers as solid heroes battling an evil force. But it depicts the Christian Church as that evil force. The story line implies that the Christian Church is devoid of good and possessed by evil incarnate in the hideous form of the "gargoyle," a beast-like creature, and his squalid dark angels. The important thing to understand is that the creators of this comic book do not present the Gargoyle as the devil. No, the implicit idea conveyed is that the gargoyle represents the Christian fundamentalists who now control the Church.

What is necessary, these comic books preach, is that the "gargoyle's" hold on the Church be destroyed and removed. To carry out this task, two forces unite: the ancient Druidic sect led by a Master named "Derwyddon" and contemporary disciples of the New Age and Hindu religion, led by a man who has given his heart to a spirit called "Germain" and a guru named Vishnu Dass.

An excerpt from The Gargoyle comic book, a hideous occult tale that glorifies the New Age religion and ancient druid witchcraft.

As anyone who has studied the occult and the New Age knows, the Druids were a witchcraft religion of Britain and Gaul that predates Christianity. Stonehenge was only one of many sites where the Druidic priests practiced sorcery and sacrificed human victims to their Sun God, Hu, and to their goddess of the harvest. The Druids were a supremely evil fertility cult that worshiped the egg and the serpent. From the Druidic religion rose the magical legends and fantasy of King Arthur, Merlin, Taliesin and Camelot.

However, in *The Gargoyle* comic books, the Druids are falsely pictured as a superior true religion of great worth and value. As the comic book's hero explains, *Druid is*:

> . . . a name enshrouded in mystery and misconception. The Truth of our Sacred Way has been distorted by time--buried in a grave of fear and superstition--by the new religion that stole humankind's heart.
>
> Britain and Gaul were home to us, those long centuries ago. We were the men of the Oak, the Wise Ones. Scholars and physicians filled our ranks; astronomers, poets, musicians. We were the keepers of the Divine Secrets--mediators between men and Gods-- children of the Heavens.
>
> We lived in . . . secrecy--worshiped the sun, the moon, and the stars. We revered the faeries, gnomes, and undines. Hu the Sun God was our Father, Ceridwen, his wife, our mother. We denied death and embraced resurrection. . . . With mistletoe and serpent's egg we could cure almost any illness.
>
> O, the tests endured before an initiate could don the white robes of the priesthood. Words cannot communicate the terror and the spiritual ecstasy of such an ordeal.[1]

Jesus Does Away With the Druid Sun God Religion

The reincarnated, "pure and peaceful hero" of *The Gargoyle* comic book laments bitterly about the "One" who came and did away with the Druid sun god religion. "I grieved, I grew bitter," he says, "I walked the earth and cursed the Saviour who had blotted out the Sun."[2]

This sinister statement is an obvious reference to Jesus, whose advent resulted in the Gospel being preached and accepted in Britain and Gaul and led to the dissolving of all but a few remaining vestiges of the pagan Druid religion of the Sun God."

The Druid priest's New Age counterpart also speaks disparagingly of Christianity. First he tells of his travels in the East to Persia, India, and Nepal, looking for the true God and true religion. Then one day, he explains, he met a miraculously wise guru, Vishnu Dass (the name means the "Supreme God" in Hindi) who enlightened him as they traveled throughout India. To this "Master" he said, I pledged "my heart, my mind, my every deed."[3]

The Comic Book War Against Christianity

According to the comic books' plot, together the "good guys"--the reincarnated Druid priest who cursed Jesus because Christ did away with his Sun God religion, and the New Age follower of Hindu guru Vishnu--vow to wage war against and defeat the "Gargoyle," the evil "demon" that today has control over the Christian Church. The awful truth is that the comic books actually portray the modern-day New Age assault on Biblical Christianity.

This comic book is New Age *par excellence*. It reinforces the decadent New Age doctrine taught by almost every New Age teacher that fundamentalist, Biblical Christianity as it is practiced by today's true Church, is evil, and not Christian at all. Their preposterous claim is that the "real Jesus" believed in reincarnation and karma and also taught the unity of all religions. The New Age revision of history says that "ancient Christianity"--the religion of the Hindus and the Druids--was changed into some kind of dread fake by Peter, John, Matthew, Paul, and the other "lying" apostles after the death of Jesus on the cross.

These apostles and the early Church fathers, so the New Age whitewash goes, were nothing but deceivers and con men. Thus, New Age leaders almost universally cry out for the "restoration" of ancient pagan Christianity.

The Church of Blood

Another comic book series that uses Christianity as a focal point for its gruesome plot is *The Church of Blood*. Here's how its creators, DC Comics, describe the story line of this grotesque drama:

> The Church of Blood originated in the small European country of Zandia in the Thirteenth Century A.D. In 1202 Christian warriors of the Fourth Crusade plundered Zandia and murdered great numbers of its people. An unnamed priest led the Zandians in fighting back.
>
> The priest drove the Crusaders from his country. He then had the pit beneath his church filled with the blood of the slain crusaders. *A year later the priest bathed in the blood, which he claimed gave him strength and immortality,* and he took on the name Brother Blood. . . . He founded the Church of Blood, in which he himself was worshiped.[4]

This comic book series takes on the blackest of overtones by showing the Church of Blood as gaining worldwide membership with branches in the United

States. Members are said to hold places of power and influence in the U.S. government and in businesses, universities, and the news media.

The comic books then go on to depict the modern-day successor to Brother Blood (also called Brother Blood) as a diabolical man who fakes his own death and then stages his supposed resurrection on television. A call for world revolution follows. This is a confusing and warped plot. Is it black allegory that mocks the death and resurrection of Jesus Christ? Or does it parallel the Book of Revelation in the Bible (see Rev. 13) which prophesies that in the last days the Beast will be wounded as to death, and then miraculously recover from the wound? The alternating themes are typical of New Age teachings that mix good and evil, black and white.

But as it turns out, the comic book plot suddenly diverges widely from the Biblical account. Instead of taking over the world, Brother Blood and his Church are soon exposed as liars and cultists. Disgraced and defeated, the rebellious Brother Blood is then bundled up and escorted away to exile by a winged alien (demon), called Azreael.

Regrettably, confusing fiction with reality, these comic books may lead many impressionable kids to the conclusion that Jesus faked His own death and resurrection and that it will take a "good" alien to defeat Christ and put things right.

Clearly, the Church of Blood comic book series is an attempt to cloud the Biblical account and to twist Scripture. It also desensitizes young readers into bloody savagery and butchery.

Attacks on Christianity are Frequent

As I have documented above, attacks on Christianity and the perversion of Bible history are popular topics in today's comic books. Series promoting pro-New Age views are so numerous we could continue on and on describing a panorama of horrors. Marvel Comics, for example, has its *Fallen Angels, The Warlord, The West Coast Avengers,* and *Doctor Strange--Sorcerer Supreme* series, while DC Comics presents its *Millennium* series.

On the cover of *The West Coast Avengers* comic books is a picture of a ghostly white figure hovering above a scene of chaos. The headline on the cover blares out, "Ancient Egypt Rocks with Dr. Strange and the Fantastic Four." Inside, we find a scene in which the hero figure, a spirit entity, gives this explanation of a life-saving supernatural event: "I suppose you can call it a miracle . . . from one god or another."[5] The seed planted in the young reader's mind, of course, is that, while miracles and the supernatural are real, any of a number of gods may be responsible for a noteworthy miracle.

Welcome to the Millennium

The cover and contents of the comic book *Millennium* are even more unholy. The cover depicts the "ascension" of ten spirits toward the sun! Inside we are treated to a bizarre, unbiblical plot in which demonic looking aliens from outer space announce to earthlings:

> We Guardians of the Universe . . . are immortal. . . . Now is the millennium come. Now the race of earth will change and breed more change in every generation. . . . We will create the heroes for the New Age of change![6]

Like all the other comic book heroes and warriors, these Guardians of the Universe deny the Jesus of the Bible and the One God of Christianity. "Once there were many universes," they declare, "some with no supreme being at all. But this universe has *many gods*--many good and many bad! In this universe *you* must be heroes or otherwise you will not survive."[7]

(Left)
Female apparitions,
demon spirits, and
unbecoming references
to Bible prophecy are
commonplace in
today's warped comics.

The demon, Crotus,
weds his betrothed in
one of the INFERNO
comic book series.
(Right)

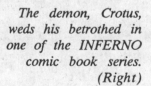

DC Comics puts in its *Millennium* comics all the New Age hocus pocus possible. The issue called "Ghostly Prelude to Armageddon" is populated by a pagan male warrior, a mother goddess spirit that rises from the waters, and a sea serpent. We also learn of crystals and their vibratory powers. The opening page provides a glimpse of the entire contents: it depicts a hostile, muscular female warrior-goddess, clothed in a black garter and swimsuit-looking outfit that glaringly reveals her ample body, astride a living tree trunk invoking the god Anu and her serpent companion. Her voice cries out:

> Let your haunting voice sing out O Sesanaga, Lava Serpent. Let its weirdling vibrations be magnified and transfigured by the mystic doom crystal that it may entice Almighty Anu, Ruler of Destiny, to slither forth from the God-plane where he has lain in wait for eons to ravage and annihilate all that has ever been![8]

The Bible tells us who the serpent is, and his name, most assuredly, is not "Sesanaga" (see Rev. 9:11 and 12:9).

Ka-Zar the Savage: Jesus' Sacrifice Defiled

Marvel Comics has outdone itself in the repugnant series called *Ka-zar the Savage*. These comic books manage to defile Christianity by visually defiling the cross of Jesus. The visual imagery is potent and kids who read these comics will undoubtedly be mentally conditioned to wrongly associate the sacrifice of Jesus on the cross with the treacherous plans of Satan and his demons.

In issue #12 of *Ka-Zar the Savage*, the beautiful mistress and consort of a devil prototype named Belasco, is shown wearing a locket around her neck. A close-up view of this locket clearly reveals an etched image of three crosses in the same arrangement as the crosses of Jesus and the two criminals on Calvary. However, what this represents is left unsaid, the image alone doing what the comic book's creator intended it to do.

As the plot unfolds, the locket is opened by the brutally evil Belasco. Inside is a magical Satanic pentagram and the beast number 666. It is explained to the reader that with this locket, the devilish Belasco plans to take over the whole world and set up his foul kingdom.

The association of the three crosses of Calvary on the outside of the locket with the pentagram on the inside leaves young readers with the unmistakable impression that somehow the crucifixion of Jesus is linked with the ages old scheme of the devil to conquer the universe.

The final scenes of this horrendous comic book reinforce this twisted association. Just as Belasco sounds the final incantation that supposedly is to result in his achieving his evil objective, a deep rumbling is heard. To the rescue comes the heroic Ka-Zar the Savage, assisted by "the elder gods," the chief of whom is a foreboding horned god. The magical locket with the three crosses and the pentagram is ripped off the neck of Belasco's mistress and thrown into the sea of boiling lava. Belasco is then destroyed. The world is again safe.

Kids reading this comic book can only come to one conclusion: that the cross, like the pentagram and the number 666, is malevolent and dark and that a resurgent paganism and the return of the "elder gods" is the only key to man's survival.

Superman and Johnny Blaze, the Ghost Rider

Even the *Adventures of Superman* comics are today being transformed into propaganda tools for the New Age Plan. In one recent issue, Superman tangles with a character named "Doctor Stratos." In the end, Stratos is defeated and tossed into the sea to perish. But not so quick. This is the New Age version, remember? Therefore, we find the submerged Stratos erupting into a boiling energy that causes the waters to churn and roar, and smoke to billow from the water's surface.[9]

Then, suddenly, Stratos bursts forth from his watery grave. "It is as I have always known," he exults, "The power is now *inside* me. I have claimed my proper destiny. The human Doctor Stratos is gone. Now Stratos, the God, walks the earth!"

While Doctor Stratos has been transformed into a New Age God, in Marvel Comics' *The Ghost Rider*, kids are acquainted with the saga of heroic Johnny Blaze. "Once not so long ago," the story line informs us, Johnny Blaze

> . . . was the pawn of Satan. He has since been freed. But for reasons he cannot yet comprehend, he still possesses Satan-spawned strength and the searing touch of hell fire. Whether these supernatural powers are a blessing or a curse, he does not know. Yet.[10]

Obviously, this scenario does not line up with Biblical Truth. First, we note that according to the comic book, "Johnny Blaze" is not freed from Satanism by Jesus but by some other unidentified power. Then we are told that although freed, he still "possesses Satan-spawned strength and the searing touch of hell fire." This is not what happens in true deliverance, because when God delivers a person and the demons are cast out, the newly cleansed person will absolutely *not* continue to possess these Satanic powers.

Finally, the comics tell us that although he is still under Satan's spell, Johnny Blaze does not yet know whether this is a blessing or a curse. The suggestion, of course, is that possessing Satanic powers may be either good *or* bad. This attempts to blot out the undeniable Biblical distinction between darkness and light, good and evil.

Arise, Spirits of the Dead!

In one of the *Ghost Rider* comics, "Wail of the Wind Witch," the character Johnny Blaze comes into contact with all manner of occult happenings. Worse, he is frequently transformed into a demon called "Ghost Rider" and sets about doing wonderful, altruistic and heroic good deeds. Indeed, this plot of demonic transformation is common to all the comic books in this series.

In one episode, we witness a live seance in which a psychic (Johnny Blaze's gentle Aunt Olga) conjures up a spirit from the dead. The spirit identifies itself as Clorhilde, a young girl from centuries ago who learned the art of "white magic" from her father, "a wise and worldly sorcerer." She claims that her sorceress powers were used only for the good of all mankind; but the populace was envious and despised her. So, unfairly and inhumanely, she had been put to death.

Later, the spirit from the dead known as Clorhilde assists "Aunt Olga" in conducting a Satanic ceremony and ritual, complete with a Satanic pentagram painted on a wooden floor, candles, and incantations to the spirits to arise and come forth.

A New Age Fantasy: Arion, Lord of Atlantis

The legend of Atlantis is prominent in New Age literature. New Age occult teachers such as Ruth Montgomery, Edgar Cayce and many others have argued vehemently that there really was an ancient continent of Atlantis. There, on Atlantis, mankind was supposedly perfected into gods. Technology and knowledge had reached high levels. The religion and worship of the Sun God and the Mother Goddess was said to hold a prominent and privileged place in the lives of Atlanteans. Atlantis was a teeming metropolis of wonders and awe until . . . the flood.

One day, the occult legend goes, disaster struck. The entire continent of Atlantis sank beneath the sea. But according to occult New Age teachings, the High Priests and Priestesses of the Atlantean religion managed to gather their holy scrolls, idols and religious artifacts and load them into the few navigable boats that remained.

They took these writings and religious paraphernalia and settled in faraway lands in Greece, Rome, Britain, Gaul (now France), Scandinavia, and elsewhere. Thus were founded the Mystery Religions, the religions based on pagan mythologies, the Druid witchcraft religious sect and others--all based originally on Atlantean holy teachings.

Arion, Lord of Atlantis, is loaded with New Age occultism.

Combine this legendary Atlantis with another occult teaching--that the star constellation Orion is the habitat of *Satan*--and you have a neat formula for New Age-oriented comic books. So it is no accident that DC Comics publishes their series called *Arion, Lord of Atlantis.*

Arion, Lord of Atlantis is jam-packed with remarkable occultism and New Age religious philosophies. Arion, we learn, has a darkly evil brother who hates him (paralleling other occult literature, such as the *Book of Mormon* of

Mormonism, which contends that Lucifer and Jesus are "brothers") and is engaged in perpetual warfare against him. But Arion manages to stay alive regardless, thanks to the mighty power of his crystals, in which the mystic spirit of his dead "Father" resides.

Presenting Kali, the Mother Goddess

This comic book series also introduces us to a Mistress, or Mother Goddess type, named "Kali." Kali is depicted as a sensitive, loving, and good nurturer who nurses Arion back to health after the epic battle with his brother. Kali is shown to be a dark haired woman with a huge circular *red mark* on her forehead.

Again, this is not by accident. Today, the Hindus in India continue to be devout worshipers of the Mother Goddess Kali. She is shown in paintings on temple walls and otherwise in artists' conceptions as a dark haired Indian woman with a red mark on her forehead--just as the comic book *Arion* depicts. The red mark indicates the location and operation of Kali's Third Eye, the Mind's Eye. This is a common mark that Hindu women, gurus and monks wear to indicate their Third Eye is open and that they are on their way or have already been transformed into all seeing, enlightened human gods.

Satanic Symbols, the Horned God, the Prince of Darkness

The occultism in *Arion, Lord of Atlantis* does not, however, end with its introduction of Kali. This entire comic book is steeped in darkness. The mind of the youthful reader is immersed with symbols. There is the Satanic triangle with the circle inside it, the winged, horned god on the altar, and the chanting and incantations to the Prince of Darkness to come forth:

Come forth, O Darkling prince, and reclaim the realm
rightfully yours since time did dawn. Come, O darkling
prince. Your followers await.[11]

Mystical Witches, Red Goddesses, Mistresses of the Martial Arts, and other Comic Book Sex Queens

She calls herself *Ms. Mystic*. She is a sexy, curvy, buxom
platinum-blond heroine who wields a magical sword and
angrily declares that the pollution and defilement of
Mother Earth's environment must stop . . . or else.
"From this day onward," she solemnly announces, "the
Planet Earth is under MY protection. Defile it not or
suffer the wrath of Ms. Mystic."

Ms. Mystic is only one of a bevy of beautiful, well-
shaped New Age starlets who adorn our kids' comic
books. There's also Amethyst, Princess of Gemworld;
Samuree, Mistress of the Martial Arts; Johnni Thunder,
a/k/a Thunderbolt; Dr. Midnight; Flare; the Red Sonja;
Frances Kane; Fury; and Goldstar; among many others.
All of these fantasy comic book heroines have one thing
in common: they are endowed with magical New Age
occult powers. Most are given to expressing New Age
religious and social doctrines in the pages of their comic
books. Quite a few wear amulets or use talismans that
protect from "evil" or enhance their supernatural
powers.

A Reincarnated Witch Comes Back

Ms. Mystic is the classic New Age type. As her comic
books tell the story, she comes to earth as a reincarnated
former witch who was cruelly burned at the stake in
Salem, Massachusetts by evil schemers. Actually, she
explains to readers, she was merely a good "white" witch
who used her powers to help people, curing them of
illnesses and disease.

I was three hundred years ago a witch. Hear me . . .
please. They called me a witch. I was a sensitive child,
sensitive to everything. . . . All living things. I could help
people without them knowing it. I didn't want to be
noticed. . . . The townspeople found me out. . . . They put
me to the stake.

I don't know how to describe this to you . . . but I
removed my *essential* body from my *mineral* body, and I
injected myself into another dimension. Once there I
was alive, but trapped and helpless . . . for three hundred
earth years, hoping, praying for someone, something, or
some force to release me. . . . Finally . . . I was able to
come home.[12]

*Ms. Mystic is the story of a reincarnated Salem witch who
comes back as a heroine to avenge Mother Earth of the
pollution to her environment.*

In the plot of this occultic comic book series, Ms.
Mystic is aided on her mission by a team of strange
experts and specialists who also possess unusual powers.
Two are supermen types who wear a costume with

occultic triangles on their chest. One wears the triangle pointed downward, the other with it pointing upward. The meaning of these two symbols is never explained; however, occultists point out that this symbolizes the union of the god and goddess, good and evil, creation and destruction, Jesus and Satan. This is also known as yin/yang, the principle of the union of opposites.

Amethyst, New Age Princess of Gemworld

The creators of *Amethyst, Princess of Gemworld,* approach the New Age from a different perspective than *Ms. Mystic* though it is just as lethal spiritually to our children. This is a continuing saga of a young, ordinary teenage girl, Amy, who has a hidden life as Amethyst, a powerful goddess type who performs heroic feats in a New Age domain somewhere far off in a magical dreamworld dimension.

The young fans of Amethyst have their minds filled with such fantasies as astral travel, magical swords, transformation of spirits into birds, and a beastly horned creation resembling Lucifer who is called Sardonyxx.

Red Sonja and the Goddess Religion

In *Red Sonja,* the comic book creators present young readers images of a legendary warrior-woman from an ancient pagan era. Red Sonja is favorably proclaimed to be the "she-devil with a sword." In one episode, she rescues a woman named Zora from the clutches of a group of beast-men. Zora is described as the "last survivor of the cave-dwelling, Red-goddess worshiping tribe, "The Favored."[13]

In yet another episode, as the shapely Red Sonja battles rival pirates of an attacking ship, she cries out to the heavens, "Red Goddess, guide my hand." Then later, after she has won the battle, Red Sonja bids farewell to her friends thusly: "Good bye Kirkos . . . and you, Menina. May the gods go with you."

Heroine Red Sonja wears a medallion around her neck that mysteriously seems to change back and forth from the image of the lightening bolt, an ancient occultic sign of Lucifer, to what appears to be the sun sign.

Johnni Thunder, Supernatural Thunderbolt of Nakedness

The comic book series Johnni Thunder, a/k/a/ Thunderbolt tells a more contemporary story.[14] Johnni Thunder is a female private eye who is magically transformed into a living thunderbolt of lightning after she is accidentally zapped by a laser generator. This miracle occurs while she is holding a golden idol of an ancient goddess in her hands.

The transformed Johnni becomes "Thunderbolt," a heroine who can fly and wage battle using bursts of lightning exploding from her fingertips.

This comic book series not only uses raw language harmful to youth, but titillatingly shows the heroine as a curvy *naked* woman of demonically-charged proportions."

Playboy, Penthouse and Samuree

Though provocative, the naked and wild image of Johnni Thunder is mild compared to the incredible array of pornographic poses kids find in each and every issue of Samuree, Mistress of the Martial Arts. In all my research I have yet to discover another comic book more alluring and lewd than Samuree. This sexy comic book character, scantily clad in tight black leather boots and shirt with only a patch of delicate material covering the buttocks and pelvic areas, is featured in a variety of sexual poses.

The comic book series, SAMUREE, MISTRESS OF THE MARTIAL ARTS, is a shockingly graphic example of sexual exploitation of our kids.

The varied physical poses of Samuree are more becoming of
PENTHOUSE and PLAYBOY magazines than children's
comic books.

The effects on a young boy of reading the salacious, graphically shocking *Samuree* comic books can only be to scar and etch his mind and turn him on to other pornographic materials. I do not believe a boy can view these sexually suggestive pictures and not be drastically and permanently marred and debased in his thoughts about sexuality. The sad thing is that Samuree combines gross violence with its sexual imagery, further warping the mind.

"This'll Bring Out the Beast in You!"

Samuree and *Johnni* are joined by a number of other comic book heroes and heroines in promoting sex and violence themes. On the cover of one of the Marvel Comic Book series, *X Factor,* is a young, pretty woman in a sexually suggestive pose. She is shown standing in front of a character tied up in chains. Teasingly, she begins to strip. Opening her shirt and lifting up her hands so he can get a good look, she coos, "I guarantee it, Iceman, this'll bring out the beast in you!"

The Ravages of Comic Book Porn

The disease of pornography spread through comic books is designed to ravage family values and mangle the minds of our youth. The comic book overlords evidently hope to capture a wide audience by promoting unhealthy and premature sexual desires in kids six, eight, nine and ten years old. This is pornography in comic book form which aims to grip the youngest of minds.

One shudders to think of how young people raised on this new type of unsavory kiddie porn will develop as they age into adulthood. What is being created is an entire new future generation of adults gradually fed and hardened to the grossest types of pornography.

The sexual suggestion on this cover is typical in today's comic books.

Both the supernatural and the carnal are combined in this comic book series.

The female dominator theme is prominent in many comic books. Note in the INFERNO issue above the baby to be sacrificed to devils. Note, too, the sexually provocative poses and dress.

If this comic book trend continues, society will see a shocking increase in rapes, mutilations and other sexual crimes. Indeed, soon we will likely be seeing a plague of news reports about teenagers and even kids eight, nine or ten sexually assaulting other youngsters.

From Comic Books to Bound Books

Comic books possess a unique element--that of visual imagery. This element is powerful and can be used for good or evil. In the next chapter, we will examine the New Age invasion of yet another arena of the child's life: the realm of books, the kind of books on the shelves of libraries or available at the local bookstore. Like comic books, some bound books also combine pictures with words, while others paint pictures with words. In either case, books or comic books, the goal of Satan's New Age conspirators is to invade the minds of our kids. Their success in the endeavor is both staggering and frightening.

TEN

Satan's Bookshelf: Dark Verses, Underground Rhymes, and Bed-Time Stories for Little Witches

Many of them also, which used curious arts brought their books together, and burned them before all men: and they counted the price of them, and found it fifty thousand pieces of silver. So mightily grew the Word of God and prevailed. (Acts 19:19, 20)

We worship the goddess Mother Nature. The devil is a Christian god. We don't have a devil. Christianity is anti-reading, anti-science, anti-learning. They are pro-Bible. You can build a pretty stupid nation like that. . . . If they would read more than one book it would help. (Z Budapest, Witch, **Guest Speaker for Children's Library Program**)

What evil lurks within the confines of elementary, junior high school, and public libraries? Plenty! Satan is having a field day with our kids, producing books of terror--books for children and teens with only one express purpose: to putrefy and trash mind and soul.

If this seems to you at first thought a harsh judgment, just wait . . . wait until you see the documentation and evidence presented in this chapter. You will be shaken, startled and disgusted. I hope also that you will be filled with loathing and anger--anger because, like me, you love children and it literally breaks your heart to see them willfully mangled and tragically abused in spirit.

It is with fantasy stories and the misuse of the imagination that Satan's New Age Masters seek to entangle our children in a massive, spidery web of occultism. Children have always been highly susceptible to fantasies and fairy stories, to amazing flights of the imagination. Childhood is an especially vulnerable period of life, and the influence of fantasy on young minds is great.

Beware of Vain Fantasies and Fables

For centuries, Godly men and women of good will have warned parents of the dangers of fantasy on youthful spirits. Hugh Rhodes' *Book of Nurture* (1554) cautioned parents "to keep them (children) from reading of feigned fables, vain fantasies and wanton stories . . . which bring much mischief to youth." Later, in the 19th century, there were many reformers like Mrs. Trimmer who, in her magazine, *The Guardian of Education,* roundly denounced the fairy stories and Mother Goose as "only fit to fill the heads of children with confused notions of wonderful and supernatural events, brought about by the agency of imaginary beings."

As we shall soon see, it would today be a good thing if parents were to embrace some of the same views as the early reformers. Sadly, fantasy and fable are now so popular and so widely received that even Christian fiction fantasy novels for kids are in vogue. It is a fact, however, that stamping the label "Christian," on a book does not sanctify it. Many so-called "Christian" fantasy novels and tales are deceptively authored by the Prince of Darkness himself.

This chapter should not be viewed as a broadside attack on *all* works of fiction. Certainly, there is room in God's Kingdom for holy stories that exercise a child's sense of awe and stretch the imagination. But in all cases, the means must justify the end and vice versa. *In other words, as a whole, a work must glorify our Lord and, in addition, its contents in their entirety should be edifying to God.* This important criterion can neither be waived nor neglected.

The worst of Satanically inspired kids' books take on religious or spiritual--sometimes even "Christian"--themes but then slyly and cunningly move the young reader into an imaginary realm of darkness. Invariably the youth does not understand the subtlety and uncanny perverseness inherent in such books. These books are often exciting, adventurous, and thrilling, and this is what captures the child's keen interest. Yet a ghostly, unseen shadow hangs about.

Many times, even mature adult Christians find difficulty in discerning the true nature of these books, craftily written as they are to secretly and imperceptibly implant sinister thoughts and suggestions contrary to the Word of God.

The best way to understand the New Age assault on our kids through books is to thoroughly review a number of titles. As we do, look for the gaping discrepancies between what these books are conveying to our kids and what God wishes to be imparted to children. The gulf, or chasm, is often great.

Witchcraft in Kids' Books

Witchcraft is on the rise throughout the world. My own estimate is that there are perhaps five to seven million active witches in America today and another thirty-five million or so persons who have studied or dabbled in witchcraft but who are not now practicing witches. The practitioners and followers of witchcraft constitute a sizeable group--a group that is exerting influence in many areas of society. The publishing of children's books is no exception.

Christian parents in San Jose, California learned the hard way how powerful the witch lobby is in the publishing of kids' books. Alarmed that San Jose's Santa Teresa Public Library was to present a presentation for kids by Z. Budapest, a famous, internationally known witch, a number of Christian parents flooded the library and city council with complaints, all to no avail.[1]

The librarian in charge of the youth section at the library scoffed at the complaining parents. "The program is informational, educational *entertainment*," she insisted. Books on witchcraft are so popular with young people, she said, that the library cannot keep them on the shelves. Most of the interest, the librarian reported, is in black magic. The witches' philosophy is "a very positive philosophy of life," she added.[2]

Is the San Jose public librarian correct? Is the religion of witchcraft *positive*? The answer is yes. Yes, witches are *positively* behind the growing tide of malignancy and darkness! Their religion preaches hatred and intolerance toward Christianity. As Z Budapest herself remarked, when questioned as to her views:

> We worship the goddess Mother Nature. The devil is a Christian God. We don't have a devil. . . . Christianity is anti-reading, anti-science, anti-learning. They are Pro-Bible. You can build a pretty stupid nation like that. . . . If they would read more than one book it would help.[3]

"I was just shocked that a public place would allow this," said one mother, who learned about the scheduled program from a flyer brought home from the library by her 13-year-old. "These people are supposed to be setting a good example."[4]

New Age Books for Kids Get High Marks

The New Age, however, is not concerned with setting a good example. It is dedicated to ruining and poisoning our kids' minds. New Agers in positions of authority in the book world are even bestowing the highest literary awards on the authors of witchcraft and other occult books. In Boulder, Colorado, an 11-year-old boy was given the book, *The Headless Cupid*, by his school library. This book favorably tells the story of a young girl who is practicing to be a witch. Alarmed, an adult neighbor of the boy visited the school, Whittier Elementary, and inquired. "Why, the book won the prestigious Newberry Honor Award and meets very strict school guidelines," he was informed.[5]

"Strict school guidelines?" *The Headless Cupid*, according to one reviewer, "contains many graphic descriptions of occult practices and effectively teaches our youth how to enter into witchcraft. This book makes the occult exciting and mysterious. The reader is never told the danger of fooling with the occult."[6]

Parents concerned about the book have cited its coverage of familiar spirits, seances, initiation rites, stealing, deceit and lying, alienation from and mistrust of parents, and the giving of unholy spiritual names. Yet, because it has won the secular world's vaunted Newberry Honor Award, practically every school and public library system in America will have this book for kids on its shelves.

Little Witch's Big Night

The Headless Cupid is by no means the only witchcraft book for kids. A most horrific example of bad taste is the book Little Witch's Big Night.[7] This book is billed by its publisher, Random House, as a "Step into Reading" book for grades 1-3. It tells of a little girl witch who cheerfully takes four young trick-or-treaters (including one in a devil costume) for a halloween ride on her broom. The book makes the witches, including Little Witch's Mother Witch, into genuinely likeable characters, again without so much as a hint of the true nature of witchcraft. Nor does the book mention the occultic roots and Satanic Druidic history of Halloween as a pagan Druidic holiday.

Which Witch?

A book by Scholastic for older kids is even more lacking in good taste. In fact, this one horrified me when I reviewed it because it accurately--and glamorously-- depicts many of the worst aspects of witchcraft and Satanism. Entitled Which Witch?, the plot revolves around a handsome young man named Arriman, who needs a wife. So he decides to hold a contest to find the loveliest and most powerful witch in town and make her his wife. "May the best witch win!" exclaims the back cover of the book.[8]

The winner of the Best Witch contest turns out to a be gorgeous young witch named Belladonna who demonstrates superior occult powers by bringing a "charming," nonrepentant, multiple wife killer back from the dead. Here is how, in part, the conjuring up ritual is described:

> So Belladonna stepped forward to the table with its long cloth and candlesticks and skull. . . .Then she took a pin from her other pocket and jabbing it into her finger, let a

drop of blood fall, like a red pearl, into the incense
pot. And immediately there was a flash, and a sheet
of rose and amethyst and orange smoke rose almost
to the roof. . . .

"Let there be darkness!" said Belladonna. . . .
Then she took up the hollow skull and walked over to the
magic triangle that Terence had chalked out for her. . .
"Do you hear me Shades of the Underworld!" cried
Belladonna, raising the skull.[9]

Books promoting witchcraft are designed for kids of all ages.

Pocket Books, another major publisher, has also en-
tered the witchcraft kids' sweepstakes with its own book,
The Witches of Hopper Street. This book is especially despicable because it encourages young girls and boys alike
to actively practice witchcraft. The back cover of the
book furnishes us a glimpse of its seemingly playful--yet
potentially foreboding--contents:

When Rae Jean Greeley invites everyone to her party
except Kelly, Jennifer, and Adelaide, Kelly and her

friends form a secret witch coven. They hold esbats (witch meetings) under a full moon, stir up magic potions--and decide to put a hex on Rae Jean's party.

But jinxing the party turns out to be a lot of trouble. Kelly's brother and his friend spy on the girls and insist on joining the coven--as warlocks![10]

The Egypt Game and other Pagan Adventures

In the same vein as *The Witches of Hopper Street* is *The Egypt Game*, by Zilpha Snyder. This is another one of those award winning Newberry Honor Books, so watch out! It is also published by Dell, the same publisher as *The Headless Cupid*, and is written by the same author.

An increasing number of books instruct children on the ancient, unholy religions of Egypt, the Americas and the Orient.

The Egypt Game capitalizes on the New Age's mania for anything ancient Egyptian, especially anything related to the unholy Egyptian religious worship of the Sun God and the Goddess. It tells of six young teens who stumble upon a deserted storage yard behind an antique and curio shop. After school and on weekends they all meet to wear costumes and role play as gods, hold evil ceremonies at an altar devoted to the Satanic Egyptian god, Set, work on their secret code, and use occultic Egyptian symbols as their names.[11]

The danger here is apparent. To role play as an ancient deity and to conduct occultic rituals is to invite demons to come and take up habitation. Yet *The Egypt Game* creates in its readers a mysterious yearning and desire for doing exactly this.

Another kids' book, *Secret of the Sun God*, encourages experimentation by youngsters ten and up in the ancient religion of the Aztecs in Mexico.[12] The Aztecs, like the Egyptians, also worshiped the Sun god. Both they and the Egyptians practiced human sacrifice and held the serpent to be sacred. These are also ideas and concepts familiar to anyone who has studied the New Age religion.

How Kids Learned to Love the Big Bad Dragon

Dragons are a popular topic in books for kids. But the dragon of old--the dreaded, fire-breathing monster of legendary dimensions--has changed his scales, so to speak. In the New Age make-over, he becomes kind, gentle, peaceful, and loving. Kids are being taught to *love* the big bad dragon. It is interesting to contrast this new, nicer version of the dragon with the Biblical account, which compares the dragon to Satan, even labeling the dragon *as* Satan:

> And the great dragon was cast out, that old serpent,
> called the Devil, and Satan, which deceiveth the whole
> world: he was cast out into the earth, and his angels were
> cast out with him (Rev. 12:9).

In the DRAGONS OF NORTH CHITTENDOM a young boy and a dragon communiate through psychic powers to bring to the world a New Age of peace and love between dragons and men.

The New Age version is viewed by kids close-up in the book *The Dragons of North Chittendon,* by acclaimed author Susan Fromberg.[13] The story is about a state of war that exists between humans and dragons. At its center is the friendship between Arthur, a peace-loving dragon and Patrick, a courageous young boy whom Arthur the dragon contacts through visualization. Patrick does not agree with his fellow humans. He does not believe that war should be waged against dragons. He longs and dreams of a "New Age" in which dragons and men will exist side-by-side in harmony. The dragon is also a kind peace-lover. As a result, dragons and men become united in peace and the world is changed forever for the better.

This is quite a departure from the Truth of the Bible. God's Word teaches that the dragon (Satan) will eventually be cast into the lake of fire and brimstone, his infernal residence for eternity (Rev. 20:10).

Service to Satan: Is It Acceptable to God?

A prime example of how a fantasy novelist is able to weave truth and untruth and fact and fable, thus distorting God's Word, is found in the C.S. Lewis book *The Last Battle*, of *The Chronicles of Narnia* series. Young people who read this book are falsely led to believe that *all the sin and evil that a person has committed serving Satan can in the end be counted as service rendered to God!*

> Then I fell at his feet and thought, Surely this is the hour of death, for the Lion (who is worthy of all honour) [supposedly the Narnian representation of Christ] will know that I have served Tash [supposedly the Narnian representation of Satan] all my days and not him. . . . But the Glorious One bent down his golden head and . . . said, Son, thou art welcome. But I said, Alas, Lord, I am no son of thine but the servant of Tash. He answered, Child, all the service thou hast done to Tash, I account as service done to me.[14]

Is Christianity a "Myth?"--The Gospel of Madeleine L'Engle

Another New Age writer of fantasy children's books who has great support in the Christian community is Madeleine L'Engle. Norman Vincent Peale's *Eternity* magazine, favorably reviewing her *A Cry Like a Bell*, wrote: "In these poems Madeleine L'Engle continues her chosen work of *retelling* the stories of the *Christian myth*."[15] This book, published by a Christian press, Harold Shaw Publishers, is chock-full of hideous suggestions. L'Engle approvingly presents the Virgin Mary as a focal point for ecumenical unity. In a theologically flawed poem called *Isaac*, she gives us this startling passage:

From now on, no fathers are to be trusted. . . .
   I know.
   I felt the knife at my throat
      before the angel stopped my
      father's hand[16]

Worse still is L'Engle's pantheistic, animistic assertion that "my father's, and the son/and the ram caught by the horns are one."[17] Then, she takes her heresy one step further to demean Jesus' deity and his sacrifice for the sins of the world. She does so by substituting the typical New Age view that Jesus' death was an initiation process. This is demonstrated in her statement that "death was not his sacrifice, but birth."[18] The Gospel of John (Chapter 1) clearly teaches the opposite--that Jesus is God, was and shall always be God, and is eternal. He was not "born again" at the cross and his physical death was not an initiation but instead was a *propitiation* for our sins.

Madeleine L'Engle has been amply rewarded for her service to Satan's New Age. Her works have won numerous literary awards, including the Newberry Medal Book, American Library Association Notable Book, The American Book Award and so on.

"Christianity Demands Enormous Imagination"

"Christianity demands *enormous imagination*" says L'Engle.[19] Her idea of imagination, however, may be far more than the souls of our kids can bear. L'Engle's books are populated with dozens of New Age occult symbols, witches, unicorns, pegasus, crystal balls, rainbows, demons, all seeing eyes, dragons, and the powers of the mind.

The covers of Madeleine L'Engle's books provide all the proof necessary for parents to send up the red flag. A *Swiftly Tilting Planet* depicts a child riding a white, pegasus unicorn horse across the sky. *A Wind in the Door* has kids standing and viewing a strange bird/man figure permeated with an array of scary, all seeing eyes. For the ghostly cover of *A Wrinkle in Time*, the same children are astride a huge, bald-headed centaur (half man/half horse) beast which has a rainbow coming from his body.

Award winning books by Madelene L'Engle are packed with New Age and pagan imagery and concepts.

Is the Bible Simply a "Story Book?"

Like the writings of C. S. Lewis, those of Madeleine L'Engle are much revered by New Agers. Given her views and the mystical and occult nature of her books, one can understand why. Though she is also popular among Christian groups--especially liberals and moderate evangelicals--she does not hesitate to let people know of her unbiblical views. L'Engle has stated that "The Bible is not a moral book. . . . It is a magnificent *storybook*." The Bible, says L'Engle, "doesn't give any answers, it just tells more stories."[20] When asked if she is a "Christian writer," she responds, "I am a writer who happens to be a Christian. I am a writer first."[21]

Possibly the most revealing description of what Madeleine L'Engle truly stands for was this letter from Milton Craig published by Colorado's Eagle Forum, associated with Phyllis Schlafly, in its excellent publication, *The Forum*:

> TO THE EDITOR:
> Christian parents should be aware that Madeleine L'Engle's definition of Christianity is quite different than the Bible's. L'Engle is a self-professed New Ager and she believes that Jesus was merely a great Master (in the vernacular of Eastern religions), who once occupied the office of Christ. However, New Agers are proclaiming that a more highly evolved Christ is now in the world and will step forward when enough people have been drawn into the Peace Movement.
> The Allen County Public Library (Fort Wayne, Indiana) prepared a summary of information about L'Engle in conjunction with her recent visit to Fort Wayne. This document lists "self-realization" among this author's areas of concern. Self-realization is the ultimate of the seven chakras, or energy centers within the human body, as taught in Eastern philosophies. Shirley MacLaine achieved self-realization in her TV miniseries when she repeatedly proclaimed, "I am God."

Our local library recounts quite accurately that L'Engle works part-time at a church in New York City. She is the librarian at St. John the Divine. This New Age cathedral achieved notoriety in recent years by displaying a life-sized crucifix with a shapely, female Christ and by housing a Buddha. David Spangler is a powerful name in New Age circles and he was invited to perform a Eucharist at St. John the Divine some years ago.

Many people who have escaped the bondage of various New Age cults talk about developing an unhealthy appetite for occultism during their school-age years. I have researched New Age mysticism for more than four years and I believe that Madeleine L'Engle is the leading Pied Piper of our nation's children into the Age of Aquarius, the New Age.

The Infiltration of Christian Bookstores

Concerned Christian booksellers continue to tell me that they are deeply troubled by the plague of ungodly children's (and adult's) fantasy now infecting the Christian publishing industry as well as by recent trends in "Christian" music. Satan desires most of all to infiltrate Christian bookstores so he can poison our children's minds while trusting, unsuspecting parents are unawares. Praise God for the many dedicated Christian booksellers who are standing up for God and contending for the faith!

One such bookseller told me recently that he is forced to spend hour after hour reviewing videos, music tapes and CD's, and books because so many overtly or secretly harbor New Age and occult messages. "If Christian publishers would employ discerning editors who know their Bible and love the Lord Jesus Christ and His Word," he agonized, "I wouldn't have to spend all my time doing this. It's just awful."

Intervarsity Press and Its Spirit Flyer Series

One book this man threw out was a "Spirit Flyer" book series, authored by John Bibee and published by Intervarsity Press, a Christian publisher that got into hot water a few years ago by publishing a pro-abortion book objected to by Franky Schaefer and many other concerned Christians.

Bibee's books for kids are filled with bizarre metaphysical images and magic. One public librarian who likes Bibee's books has said that his books are perfect companions to those that tell of the pagan gods and goddesses and the Norse legends and myths.[22] She's correct. Bibee's books do acquaint his young readers with pagan religious principles hostile to Christianity. Among the worst of Bibee's Intervarsity books are *The Magic Bicycle* and *The Toy Campaign*.

Predictably, author John Bibee says that his own inspiration and influences came from C. S. Lewis and Madeleine L'Engle, both of whom, like him, specialize in New Age metaphysical fiction.[23]

The examples of C. S. Lewis, Madeleine L'Engle, and John Bibee demonstrate that in this age of deception and apostasy, it is so vitally important that we who know the Truth pray and ask God for His gift of discernment. We cannot rely on our own judgment, nor can we count on the label "Christian" any longer as a sure sign of purity and holiness. No, God is our only refuge. We must ask Him for guidance . . . and we must do so continuously. He loves us and He will not leave us to our own vain and erroneous thoughts and wonderings.

Walt Disney's "The Sorcerer's Apprentice"

The proof that discernment is desperately needed today is amply supplied by yet another book that tens of thousands--perhaps millions--of kids have read. The book,

The Sorcerer's Apprentice, comes with the blessing and label of "Walt Disney," causing many parents to accept it without question.[24]

Again, we see the fallacy of trusting in man and his works. This book is geared to arouse an inner desire in young readers for knowledge of mysticism, magic, sorcery, and witchcraft. It tells the story of a youthful apprentice (Mickey Mouse) to a great old sorcerer. The apprentice wants to do the powerful magic that the sorcerer can do; so when the old man leaves, the apprentice grabs the magical hat the sorcerer left behind and puts it on. Then he proceeds to tell a broom to go fetch water. The broom does as it is commanded but then goes berserk. Soon, it has multiplied into many brooms, all of which busily go about fetching water . . . too much water! An alarmed Mickey tells them to stop, but his magical hat no longer seems to suffice.

By the time the old sorcerer returns, the place is covered with water. It's a mess. Seeing what Mickey Mouse, his apprentice, has done, he severely scolds Mickey. "The Sorcerer looked down at his little helper: 'Don't start what you can't finish,' he said."[25]

The message the child gets from reading Walt Disney's *The Sorcerer's Apprentice* is clear. It's quite alright--even highly desirable--to be a sorcerer. But one must study and be willing to be an initiate for many months and years. It doesn't come overnight. Dabbling isn't enough. Advanced occult magic requires great preparation and the learner should not start what he can't finish.

Shel Silverstein's "Someone Ate the Baby"

Sorcery is only one tool the New Age is using to destroy our kids. Another is savage, gross violence and cruelty. Consider this black, supposedly humorous poem for kids from award winning author Shel Silverstein's bestselling kid's book *Where the Sidewalk Ends.*

Dreadful
Someone ate the baby, it's rather sad to say.
Someone ate the baby, so she won't be out to play.
We'll never hear her whiney cry
or have to feel if she is dry.
We'll never hear her asking, "Why?"
Someone ate the baby.
Someone ate the baby, it's absolutely clear.
Someone ate the baby, 'cause the baby isn't here.
We'll give away her toys and clothes,
We'll never have to wipe her nose,
Dad says, "That's the way it goes,"
Someone ate the baby.
Someone ate the baby, what a frightful thing to eat.
Someone ate the baby, though she wasn't very
    sweet.
It was a heartless thing to do,
the policemen haven't a clue,
I simply can't imagine who,
would go and (burp) eat the baby.[26]

There can be little doubt that we are raising our kids up to be monsters. Adolph Hitler and his jack-booted Nazi gestapo would be proud of the progress we are making in America in raising our kids to thrive on chaos, meanness, and inhumane acts of butchery.

Nancy Drew to Titillate Young Readers

Parents who care about their daughters have also noticed the new free sexual direction of books and magazines aimed primarily at young teenage girls. For example, millions of adults are intimately familiar with the *Nancy Drew*, fictional sleuth series of books. Well, in 1986 Simon & Schuster, America's second largest publisher, announced that the old Nancy Drew was "dead." She was being replaced by a new "rejuventated" Nancy Drew character--a more sexy, titillating Nancy Drew. The new heroine, said the publisher, will be "sexy in a low-key way." She will, they boasted, wear tightfitting designer jeans, show a little cleavage on book covers, "ogle gorgeous boys," and have difficulty controlling her sexual urges.[27]

The "new, improved," more worldly image of Nancy Drew is indicative of where the New Age and secular humanist Masters of publishing want to take our youth. Nancy Drew was once the epitome of the clean-cut intelligent, kind, all-American, virtuous girl next door-- the girl every teen wanted to be. But now comes the revamped, sexually active teen role model, with an image more in keeping with the "anything goes" morality of the New Age.

Just how far the New Age has come in providing kids this anything goes, more-worldly image will become painfully apparent in the chapter that follows, "Mighty Mouse Snorts Cocaine!"--Hey Kids, It's Show Time!

"Mighty Mouse Snorts Cocaine!" -- Hey Kids, it's Show Time!

For the weapons of our warfare are not carnal,
but mighty through God to the pulling down of
strongholds. Casting down imaginations, and every
high thing that exalteth itself against the knowledge
of God, and bringing into captivity every thought to
the obedience of Christ. (II Cor. 10:4, 5)

Let us . . . build our new world first in that place from
which all great creations spring--the realm of the
soul's inspiration--the eye of the mind.
(Vera Alder,
When Humanity Comes of Age)

Teenager Mark Branch was fascinated by the blood, gore and insanity of slasher movies. He was especially fond of Jason, the crazed slasher in the *Friday the 13th* horror films. Mark had watched the Jason videos again and again, observing how the monstrously brutal killer carefully stalked and savaged his victims. Finally, it was all to much for him.

Today, Sharon Gregory is dead. Mark Branch, inspired by his celluloid role model, Jason, the beast, ambushed and repeatedly stabbed the young college student he had chosen as his first victim. Days later, a deer hunter also found the body of Mark Branch. The police in Greenfield, Massachusetts say that the deranged young man had hung himself from a tree.[1]

What is it about a movie or a television show that would so captivate and twist the mind of a young person that he would then go out and commit such heinous acts? Just how damaging to a child's soul *are* TV and movies? And to what extent is the New Age responsible for the incredible trash now common fare on our screens?

The Shocking Effects on the Mind

It's for sure that TV and movies severely impact the minds of viewers, especially of children. In Dallas last year, a man who brutally murdered three people with a hatchet calmly told police that the murders did not bother him much because "it's just like watching a movie or something."[2] Frank Titioni, a criminal attorney defending a young girl who had killed her nine-year-old sister, told TV interviewer Larry King that the girl was not responsible for her act because since the age of nine, she had immersed herself in reading demon and horror novels and seeing movies on these subjects. Finally, he explained, the movie *Bad Seed* inspired the young teenager to murder her own sister.

Victor Streib, attorney and author of the book, *Death Penalty for Juveniles*, told *U.S.A. Today* that after studying 281 cases of murder by teenagers, he came to this conclusion:

> Kids act from impulse. . . . They don't know what death really means. They're quite honestly surprised the victim is dead forever, because on television, and in the movies and in the books, they're not dead forever.[3]

Today's movies for kids often reflect the most savage forms of cruelty and bloodshed.

At what age are children at risk from watching bad TV or movies? Researchers have found that infants as young as ten months are able to learn from what they're seeing on television. In one study, scientists said that a baby can learn to disassemble a novel toy from watching television. Between one and two years of age, infants can already make sense of a show like *Sesame Street.*[4]

Imagine how many tens of thousands of scenes of butchery and violence, sex, sorcery, and occultism are seen by the average child during, say, the first 12 years of life alone, and you begin to realize the gravity and seriousness of what is happening to our kids. For example, one study found that television viewers are bombarded with an average of 27 scenes per hour on both daytime and prime-time TV discussing sexual behavior or performing sexual acts. In one season alone, 65,000 references to sexual behavior were broadcast. Sixty-five thousand![5]

The New Age is Pleased

The New Age leadership is not at all discouraged by what is happening to our children as a result of sorcery, barbarism and sex on TV. They applaud it. Especially satisfying to New Agers are movies and shows which teach kids about mythical gods and goddesses and space aliens and creatures, and those that introduce them to occultism and New Age practices.

Gene Roddenberry, creator of TV's *Star Trek* and a fervent New Age critic of Biblical Christianity, believes that kids' thoughts create *reality* for them. So, he's very much in favor of New Age-oriented shows that present his kind of themes. In an essay he wrote for Volkswagen Corporation that was published as an advertisement in *Time* magazine, Roddenberry had harsh words for Christians who believe in Jesus only as well as for people who believe in American patriotism:

> Those who insist theirs is the only correct government or economic system deserve the same contempt as those who insist that they have the only true God.[6]

Understandably then, in TV's renewed *Star Trek: The Next Generation*, the spaceship's captain and crew are depicted lecturing and instructing God that he should not be so absolute in His moral demands. Meanwhile, a new interplanetary rule requires the spaceship not interfere with or attempt to change any planetary civilization's set of religious and moral values.

New Age Teachings on The Muppets Show?

The New Age disciples in charge of network and cable television programming work hard to smuggle every bit of New Age theology possible into their programs for kids. On the popular The Muppets Show, a muppet excitedly announces to Kermit the Frog, "It's here, it's here. My correspondence course. . . . 'How to be a Superhero!'" Then, turning the pages of the book he is holding, the muppet reads aloud, "Chapter Ten--How to Fly. Flying is a matter of belief. Anyone can fly as long as he believes he can."[7]

What the muppet did *not* explain to the kids, however, was *where* his producer or screenwriter got his idea for the correspondence course which teaches "How to Fly." The guru Maharishi Mahesh Yogi, "Father" of Transcendental Meditation, promises his followers that through their own mind powers, polished through meditation and visualization, they can levitate, even fly--as long as they believe they can![8]

Once we understand this connection, we also begin to comprehend why Jim Henson, producer of The Muppet Show, was the film-maker who brought to the big screen the demonically-energized J. R. R. Tolkien (Lord of the Rings) adaptation, The Dark Crystal. This also provides insight why, on a recent Muppet Show, when asked whom he would most like to be married to, the character Elmo, referring to the blasphemous female rock star, quickly answered, "Madonna, Madonna, Madonna, Madonna!"[9]

The New Age Goal: Redirecting the Media "Along Spiritual Lines"

New Age leaders are well aware of how powerful an influence they can exert over our youth through the imagery of films. And so are Satan's demons, who are directing

New Age film-making from behind the scenes. In a commentary on children, published by the New Age's *World Goodwill* organization, the authors note that due to parenting failure, children "are being raised largely through television." "We must," said the commentary, "begin to upgrade the quality of our TV programming if we are to improve the quality of our children's lives."[10]

However, what the New Age means by "quality" television programming is not at all what God's people would mean. As *World Goodwill* plainly states: "This is not to advocate the fundamentalist approach to television programming which seeks to enforce strict censorship on all information that is considered unacceptable to certain mentalities." What society needs to do, *World Goodwill* concludes is "redirect" the media "along spiritual lines."[11]

The New Age Spirits Love Today's TV and Movies

Redirecting the media "along spiritual lines" is exactly what the New Age is now busy doing. "Father Andre," a spirit channeled by Karen Glueck, medium and founder of the One World Life Service (OWLS) group in Austin, Texas, was quoted as saying:

> The type of (New Age) changes I like talking about are things like your movies. Look at the quality of your movies coming out, for example, *E.T.* and *Space Camp.* Other movies are coming out about uniting. *Out of Africa* is about (reincarnated) partners. . . .
>   You have a *Star Trek* movie about (New Age) Genesis, about a planet being transformed in the twinkling of an eye. This opens up the possibility of a miraculous transformation for your planet. So there are a lot of excellent movies being channeled now.[12]

Keep in mind that the compliment from this channeled spirit, "Father Andre" about the many "excellent
movies being channeled now" means *there are many
movie ideas and screenplays being given to New Age human disciples of Satan in Hollywood and the TV industry
by demon masters!*

Writing in the *Psychic Journal,* New Age film reviewer Sioux Rose commended the film industry for its
ingenuity and innovation in presenting New Age themes
to young people and adults. "The Aquarian Age," wrote
Rose, is bringing a new, positive dimension to films.
"Technology has amplified the capacity to spread the
dream." Rose proudly observes that even New Age *prophecies* have become the focus of movies.[13]

She has especially kind words to shower on such New
Age-oriented movies as *Raiders of the Lost Ark, E.T.,
Superman, Star Wars, Heaven Can Wait,* and *Resurrec-
tion.*

> When Luke Skywalker (in *Star Wars*) is taught to "use
> the force," it is the same force within that *E.T.* healed
> with, and indeed the same force which Ellen Burstyn's
> character (in *Resurrection*) demonstrated miracles
> through. After all, "A rose by any other name would
> smell as sweet."
>
> One could even take a film such as *Raiders of the
> Lost Ark* and see universal spiritual lessons illuminating
> within its breathtaking plot structure. The law of karma
> . . . is presented with tremendous visual impact.[14]

New Age Movie-Makers as Modern Day Prophets

According to Rose, "the film media is the *Oracle* of our
present times, and through its images, which are imprinted upon the subconscious mind, come the ideals of
our greatest spiritual prophets and teachers."[15] She suggests that the films of today are the result of the visions of

New Age teachers who are modern-day reincarnated avatars or prophets:

> Stephen Spielberg (*E.T.*) may well have been the Joseph spoken of in the bible, whose dreams inspired pharaohs, kings, and the common man alike.[16]

Who is it that inspires these modern-day, reincarnated avatars and prophets of the New Age? Sioux Rose attributes the new movies and films to the Force: "The Aquarian Age is AIR," she writes, "signifying that it works through mind and ideas and beliefs."[17]

How revealing! As Rose admits, the Aquarian Age *is* AIR, for the Bible identifies Lucifer, the overlord of the New Age religion, as *the Prince of the power of the air* (Eph. 2:2).

A Survey of the Damage Being Done

Perhaps the best way to gain a perspective of just how much damage is being done to our kids through films is to survey some of the more popular TV shows and movies. When we do, the inescapable conclusion we must reach is this: whether prime-time TV, Saturday morning and after-school cartoons and shows, or big screen movies, *nowhere* can safety be found for our children. *The realm of movies and TV is a demonic free-fire battle zone and our children are hapless targets.* If this charge sounds too incredulous, read on as we discuss the amazing case of one of children's most cherished TV heroes.

Mighty Mouse Snorts Cocaine--A National Shame

He is a kiddie show cartoon superhero, a tiny figure who swoops down out of the sky to save the day. Wearing his red and yellow super suit, he saves maidens in distress, rescues falling airplanes, and halts natural disasters. He was always viewed as spotless, incorruptible, and virtuous . . . *until April 23, 1988.* That's the day that CBS-TV depicted *Mighty Mouse* on television *snorting cocaine.*

In "The Littlest Tramp" episode of *Mighty Mouse: The New Adventure,* the cartoon hero is shown reclining beside a campfire. He is down in the dumps because the girl he loves does not return his affection. Then without warning, the hero quickly draws a handful of powder from under his cloak and inhales it through his nostrils.

It was obvious that CBS aired the Mighty Mouse episode to show that cocaine helps one overcome feeling "down." Just before sniffing the substance Mighty Mouse appears in low spirits. In the next scene he is restored to his peppy, normal self.

In an episode of TV's popular Mighty Mouse cartoon, the hero was shown reaching into his cape, pulling out and snorting cocaine.

Responding to the charges, CBS VP for program practices George Dessart ridiculously claimed that Mighty Mouse was merely snorting up his nose a mixture of flowers, strawberries and over-ripe tomatoes. Dessart remarked that the cartoon hero pulled out a "mass of crushed stems, tomatoes and flowers. . . . We see the aroma reach his nose. . . ."[18]

Expert analysis revealed the truth. A Mississippi Narcotics Agent who viewed the film was not told anything about the film prior to viewing it. Afterwards, he was asked about it. "He was sniffing cocaine," was the response. Later, U.S. Congressman Rod Chandler (R-Wash.) sent two attorneys from his staff to view the film. Congressman Chandler said his attorneys confirmed "that Mighty Mouse had indeed snorted cocaine."[19]

The man responsible for the Mighty Mouse travesty, Ralph Bakshi, created the first X-rated pornographic cartoon, "Fritz the Cat," in 1972. Playboy helped finance that pornographic cartoon.

"CBS knew about Bakshi's past when they hired him to do the Mighty Mouse cartoon series," stated Donald Wildmon, head of the American Family Association which exposed this squalid affair. "They intentionally hired a known pornographer to do a cartoon for children and then allowed him to insert a scene in which the cartoon hero is shown sniffing cocaine."[20]

Wildmon added that Judy Price, CBS Vice President in charge of children's programming, is thrilled with the opportunity to deal with controversial issues in children's programs. Price said, "I think we've broken a lot of ground [in children's programs] where people would not have dared to go in prime-time." When asked why she took over the children's programming, she replied, "I could get away with more."[21]

Unrepentant over the Mighty Mouse debacle, creator Ralph Bakshi continues on his path of wrecking our children. Interviewed on the TV news program *West 57th*

Street, he was favorably portrayed as a man who brings "satire" and "sophistication" to kids' TV cartoons. Also, after a new episode of *Mighty Mouse* was featured, called "Witch Tricks," Bakshi proudly touted its "nightmarish quality" to the *West 57th Street* interviewer.[22]

Lessons from Demons

It is increasingly clear that with precious few exceptions, Satan is in total charge of kids' TV. Most kiddie shows and cartoons are an absolute disgrace. On a Saturday morning not long ago, I turned on the TV and began to flip channels. On one network show, *Pound Puppies*, Millie, the guardian of Cooler and his pals, lay on her deathbed. The puppies gather round in tears. Bathed in light, Millie assures them, "I'll always be with you in spirit."

Later, Millie, as a spirit, does return to Cooler in a vision to take him for a ride on her magical, Pegasus winged horse.

Pound Puppies is a Hanna-Barbera production. This company also produces the *Smurf Family*, another TV cartoon series known to prominently display New Age occultism. In various episodes, Papa Smurf has used candles, Satanic pentagrams and incantations to perform magic. In other programs, the "loveable" little blue critters practice levitation and charms.

Dungeons & Dragons

I also watched an episode of the TV cartoon show *Dungeons & Dragons*, a take-off on the occult fantasy game for kids. This particular program had a "Dungeon-Master," an all-wise "Yoda" type creature, as guide and protector. He magically appeared and disappeared.

The New Age theme was that the kids try to "find their way home" (meaning: self-realization or godhood). Along the way, they meet up with all sorts of New Age occult figures and activities including dragons, bat-horses, magic, sorcery, Merlin's castle, power gems, wizards, etc. There is also a loveable little white unicorn named "Uni."

When the searching kids asked their guide, the Dungeon-Master, where *he* came from--where *his* home was, he pointed to the ground and answered, "Halfway between there and here."

Thundercats and Their Third Eye

This cartoon features the magical Eye of Thundera (the New Age and Hindus call it the Third Eye or the All Seeing Eye). Sorcery is packed into every episode. Llano, the main character, talks to his dead father, and his magical sword gravitates to his hand. The character Mumm-Ra (Ra was the Egyptian Sun God) carries cobras around with him. The young folks watching *Thundercats* discover a beast-like hero, practice yoga exercises, communicate with demon gods and more.

Such kids' programs on American TV as *He-Man, She-Ra, and My Little Pony* are wildly popular among youth in Europe, Japan, and elsewhere overseas as well. In Great Britain, Banner Ministries, the Christian publisher of the excellent newsletter *Mainstream*, recently reviewed two famous American imports. Below is a summary of what the editors had to say about *He-Man* and about *My Little Pony.*

As shown on this cover of THUNDERCATS magazine, one of the heroes is this demonic being who has a weapon of a petrified arm of a beast.

"Ascended Masters" Preparing Children for the New Age

Children are being drawn deeply into the occult world by cartoons such as *Masters of the Universe, She-Ra, Transformers,* and *Thundercats,* portraying demons and supernatural powers. New Agers believe that this world is governed from a spiritual center called Shamballa, invisible to mortal eyes, where Ascended Masters who are supposed to be highly evolved spirit-beings (actually fallen angels) make the decisions concerning our lives and future.

These Masters are working out a plan to transform "Adam" (man) into a being with psychic powers able to overthrow the rule of God. So the stories contained in the cartoons reflect this theme (and it is found in science fiction and horror movies, too.)

In the *He-Man* cartoons, we see the character Adam, a mere man, transformed into the super heroic He-Man by the mysterious power of "Greyskull" and by using the magic of his spirit-guide. Each episode shows He-Man in combat against the cohorts of the evil Skelctor. In reality, these stories prepare children to seek after the secret things of Satan, which are supernatural powers and hidden wisdom.

He-Man's magic sword and the power of Greyskull represent occult powers. The evil Lord Skeletor is all that belongs to this material plane--including the God we worship, whom the occultists believe to be a lower god about to be overthrown and superceded in the New Age of the spirit-realm. Satan always turns things upside down and reverses the truth. In essence, He-Man and his Masters of the Universe are battling against God and His Church.

He-Man and the Masters of the Universe have many parallels in New Age Occultism. Note the all-seeing eye, and also the red cross on the chest of He-Man composed of four triangles pointing to the center.

My Little Pony

For younger children, comic stories with a wide variety of rainbow colored animals have been created. These include *Gummie Bears, Care Bears, Rainbow Brite, Kypers*, and *My Little Pony*. Not only do the colors of the rainbow, a major New Age symbol, figure largely in the appearance and stories of these playthings, but the teaching is reinforced by characterization of each color. (New Agers believe that each color represents a god responsible for a certain human personality trait or activity.)

Children, in playing with toys based on these characters, quickly pick up the idea that rainbow personalities are good and helpful, and that the "rainbow-power" they use can magically transform every situation. The plots on TV and in the comics are childish adaptations of New Age doctrines. In *My Little Pony*--which should be titled *My Little Phony*--a magic sword (psychic power) is used, and various other spells, enchantments and supernatural wonders are performed.

Moreover, the ponies are shown as *unicorns* which is a potent symbol of the power of the Third Eye and of Antichrist, the little horn. Also, note the double zig-zag ("SS") near the pony's tail. This represents the *seig rune*, the pagan symbol of Satan.

Popular in TV programs for kids, the winged pegasus horse is named after the ancient goddess "Peggae" while the unicorn is a long-standing occultic beast of a dark nature.

One *Little Pony* story tells of a royal prince (Lucifer) who has been deprived of his princess (power) who has been imprisoned in the deepest dungeon (hell) by the evil Lord (God). He rescues and restores her with the help of the pony/unicorns by means of a red rose (a much-used gnostic and occult symbol representing hidden wisdom and the re-birth of the spiritual). Much more could be said about the symbolism and teaching in these comics, but it is perhaps enough just to condemn them for their blatant occultism.

She-Ra: The Incredible Awakening of the New Age Mother Goddess

A classic example of how New Age gurus have been able, with demonic help, to take symbols and practices of ancient Babylon and present them as marvelous, "with it" representations for today's youth is seen in the current fascination among kids for a feminine superbeing goddess. Right under our noses, our kids are being introduced to the Mother Goddess of ancient Babylon. Amazingly, this fulfills Bible prophecies.

She is described in the Bible as a wicked whore, a diabolical woman drunken with the blood of the saints and the martyrs of Jesus. She is depicted as a false goddess, upon whose forehead is a name written: MYSTERY, BABYLON THE GREAT, THE MOTHER OF HARLOTS AND ABOMINATIONS OF THE EARTH (Revelation 17:5, 6). She represents the unholy Mother Goddess of the ancient Babylonian religion which flourished in the days of Abraham, spreading later to Egypt, Greece, and Rome and even into far Asia and the uttermost parts of the globe.

Your kids know of this Mother Goddess. They see her as a seductive, shapely and curvaceous superwoman wielding supernatural powers and performing incredible feats of magic and sorcery. Her name, as almost every child from toddler to teen knows, is *She-Ra*.

She-Ra is today's reigning queen of kids' TV programs. Each Saturday morning millions of boys and girls thrill to her god-like exploits. In ancient Egypt, the feminine Ra reigned as a god-like queen. Ra, or Isis, was called the "Queen of Heaven" and was also worshiped by ungodly apostate Jews whose treacherous conduct in serving this false goddess of Baal kindled God's anger to wrath.

Disappearing into the woods, Princess Adora quickly drew her Sword of Protection. Magic crackled like lightning as she became She-Ra, Princess of Power, and her horse, Spirit, was changed into a mighty winged unicorn known as Swift Wind!

For the honor of Grayskull, I am She-Ra!

She-Ra with magical sword and her unicorn steed. Observe the fan-type sun sign on her tunic.
Inset, right: The Mother Goddess of Babylon, like the cartoon heroine She-Ra, also had her magical sword. (Taken from Alexander Hislop's THE TWO BABYLONS)

In the City of Babylon, the goddess was called Ashtar, queen to the bull god. Her symbol was the dragon, a symbol now being fobbed off on our kids by the New Age plotters. The sensual and desirable Egyptian goddess Ra was said to be "mistress of the gods." Her god-son's name was Horus, the Sun God, whose all-seeing eye is today prominently featured on both our U.S. one dollar bill and as a popular symbol for thousands of New Age publications and commercial items. Horus was represented as an idol by the golden calf which the children of Israel blasphemously worshiped in the desert during the temporary absence of their leader, Moses.

In male form, Ra became the "Ram," a horned goat god which even today's Satanists continue to revere. In the contemporary Hindu religion of India, we find the same Ra being called by the name "Rama" (Ra-Ma), whose name literally means "sexual pleasure."

Goddess of Dark, Demonic Forces

In ancient Egypt, this mystery religion goddess was thought to be the master of the spirit world and head of dark, demonic forces. She also had a male-god lover who shared dominion with her. Amazing as it is, the She-Ra to whom our kids are so attached is depicted on TV as reigning supreme in a spirit world called "Eternia." The winged horse she rides, named "Spirit," is magically transformed into a horned unicorn (both the winged pegasus horse and unicorn are popular New Age symbols). Just as the Egyptian god/goddess Ra was adored, today She-Ra is also adored. In fact, TV producers have even given her a secret identity: *Princess Adora.*

These astonishing parallels between the Mother Goddess of Babylon and the She-Ra of TV cartoon shows, movies and comic books fame should not surprise us. New Age leaders must be truly pleased that millions of kids are today worshiping the ancient goddess under her thinly veiled disguise as She-Ra, Princess of Power.

Kingdom Chums

This cartoon series for the younger set features stories supposedly based on Biblical events. Actually it is sacrilegious and New Age to the hilt. The very first episode was a retelling of David and Goliath. A raccoon (the animal) played the part of David. While little David faces down the giant monster, Goliath, he recites part of the 23rd Psalm, then he begins to talk about New Age concepts such as "the power within" and "believing in yourself."

Unlike the facts stated in the Biblical version, God isn't of too much help to David in this putrefied TV version. Instead of divine intervention, a weaker and smaller David is forced to trick Goliath into letting his defenses down. He does this by throwing a stick in the air to distract him. Then, while Goliath is off-guard, David zaps him.

Squire Rushnell, ABC's Vice President for children's TV, is quite proud of Kingdom Chums. Rushnell, who says that his own religious background is "very broad," is pleased that the Bible stories in the series do not offend anyone. "We take out the violence. I mean we do not show that. In the real story, Christ was nailed to the cross. We're not going to do that."[23]

The David and Goliath premier show made Rushnell especially proud. "The real value of that story," he exclaims, "was that if you believe in the power you have within you, whether you call it God or not, you can take on more formidable tasks."[24]

What we have here, friends, is "another gospel" (Gal. 1:8) being presented to our kids with raccoons and other animals helping to ease the poison down the children's throats.

Word, Inc., the giant Christian book and recording company, was the catalyst for this abomination. It was Word that first published the story book version of *Kingdom Chums* that ABC-TV later adapted for the tube. *Moreover, ABC-TV, the conglomerate, owns Word.*

This is certainly sufficient proof that *anything* Word publishes--including all kids' materials--should be looked at carefully by Christian parents. Word's records and recordings are especially suspect: this is the company that produces an entire New Age music series, deceptively calling it "Christian contemplative music."

Movie Magic: Satan Comes to Babysit Your Children

Big screen, full-length commercial movies have never been more sordidly Satanic than at this present time. The Big Screen used to be an innocent place for rib-tickling fun, wholesome spine-tingling heroism and adventure, and heart-sinking love and romance. Now, two hours at the movies often translates into two hours of occult education, and dropping the kids off at the movie theatre is about the same as letting Lucifer come into your home to babysit.

Among the recent films that contain blatant New Age occult themes are *The Golden Child, Hello Again, Starbrite and the Star-Stealer, Dune, E.T., Jewel of the Nile, 2010*, the many *Ninja* films, the *Star Wars* trilogy, *Cocoon* and *Cocoon: The Return, All of Me, The Karate Kid, Made in Heaven, Date With an Angel, The Mission, Masters of the Universe, Ghostbusters, Superman IV: The Quest for Peace, The Witches of Eastwick, Robocop, Legend*, the *Solarbabies*. The list is endless.

Perhaps the best way to examine the type of movies that Satan's New Age elite is peddling to our kids is by looking at movie director and producer George Lucas and his New Age movies. Lucas is the man who can properly be called the Pioneer of New Age Cinema.

Secrets of "Yoda" and "The Force"

In his *Star Wars* movies, including *Return of the Jedi*, New Age movie director, George Lucas cleverly brainwashes young people into believing that instead of the God of the Bible, the universe is mysteriously governed by "The Force." For example, instead of the traditional blessing, "May God be with you," Lucas substitutes, "May The Force be with you." In Lucas' vision of The Force, it is a realm where supernatural spirit beings reside and a realm in which superbeings called "Masters" can access knowledge and wisdom.

One of the *Star Wars* characters which almost every person in America, Canada, and Europe recognizes instantly is a Master named *Yoda*. Yoda is grotesque in appearance--a dwarf-like being with strangely shaped ears. But he is also portrayed as friendly and as being endowed with uncanny wisdom. Yoda is a "good," even loveable, almost God-like character who befriends Luke Skywalker, the hero character of the *Star Wars* saga.

How did George Lucas and his associates come up with the idea for Yoda? Astonishingly, I recently came across an illustration in the Satanic book, *Secret Teachings of All Ages*, that bears a remarkable resemblance to Yoda.

On page CI of this book I discovered a picture of a medieval magician conjuring up a notorious demon named "Mephistopheles." Mephistopheles is depicted as taking the Yoda-like form as he magically appears on the spot where a powerful occult symbol has been drawn with chalk on the floor of the magician's chamber. This symbol, one of the most sinister in the occult, is the Satanic triangle inside a circle. Could this be the same Yoda of George Lucas' *Star Wars*? Is Yoda in reality a demon whom Lucas attempts to instill in kids' minds as a heroic, all-knowing, all-wise "Master?"

Interestingly enough, *Secret Teachings of All Ages*, the book in which Yoda's demon look-alike appears, *was published in 1928 before Lucas was even born.* Of additional interest is the revelation that in a separate occultic book, *The Keys of Enoch, Yod* is the title given to "the finger of god." And who is the "god" of *The Keys of Enoch?* Satan. Are the *Yod* of *The Keys of Enoch* and the *Yoda* of George Lucas somehow related?

Regardless of this remarkable resemblance, we have no proof that George Lucas' Yoda and the demon pictured in *Secret Teachings of All Ages* are one and the same or that Lucas has ever read or seen this occult book. But there can be little doubt that George Lucas was inspired by a dark force in bringing Yoda to our kids.

The demon, Mephistopheles, here shown being conjured up by a magician in Manley P. Hall's 1928 occult classic bears a remarkable resemblance to Yoda, the wise ascended master of the Star Wars saga, RETURN OF THE JEDI.

What or Who is "The Force?"

George lucas' *Star Wars* deity is The Force, a mysterious, all pervasive "God" energy. This Force is simply the New Age synonym for *Lucifer*.

In his book, *The Force*, prominent New Age lecturer and author Stuart Wilde describes The Force in this manner:

> The *Force* is an energy that experiences evolution. It is massive, exhilarating, magnanimous beyond description --perhaps, you might want to call it God.[25]

The New Age and the occult labor tirelessly to convince mankind that there is no personal God who loves us. All that exists is this impersonal Force. Thus, man is himself the highest achievement of creation. Jesus Christ, therefore, was simply another man--part of The Force.

Many producers and directors, as well as writers, use the media of TV and movies to indoctrinate and propagandize our kids to New Age doctrines and concepts. Sometimes, in their haste to defame God and undermine His Word, they commit the most heinous of blasphemies. A prime example is found in the writings of Stuart Wilde. Again from his New Age text, *The Force*, we see Wilde knowingly twisting the immortal words of Jesus our Lord (John 8:32) into the following diabolically perverse formula:

> "The Force loves you.
> Love of the Force sets you free."[26]

Willow Another Satanic Film by Lucas

Following his *Star Wars* success, New Age movie director George Lucas gave us yet another mind-twisting cinema production in the movie *Willow*. Along with co-director Ron Howard (*Cocoon, Splash*) he goes about deceiving millions of youth through his thinly veiled movies which promote the New Age and the occult.

General Kael, a demonic warrior from the George Lucas movie, WILLOW. Note the two horns of his horse.

Willow is chock-full of sorcery and Biblical distortions. The movie's premise is that a baby named Elora, destined to grow up to be a "good queen of the Universe," must, through magic and sorcery, be protected against the evil designs of a dark, sinister rival.

How do we know that the baby, Elora, is the "good" queen? Because, the moviemakers say, she has the prophetic *Mark!* And though the movie's script is mute on the subject, consider her name: "Elo" stands for *Elohim* (Gods) while *Ra* is the name of the ancient Egyptian Sun God/Goddess, now revived by many in the New Age. Thus, we have Elora, or the God/Goddess Ra, who has a Mark to prove her purity and goodness. This is a direct contradiction to Revelation 13 and 17 in our Bible.

In essence, this movie glorifies the harlot religion of Babylon, whose Antichrist, the man with the number 666, will cause all the world to take Satan's hideous Mark of the Beast. Whether knowingly or unknowingly, directors Lucas and Howard are being used by the Adversary to condition our kids' minds to serve the coming Antichrist.

TWELVE

Toys that Tarnish, Games that Terrorize: The Awful Truth About Dungeons & Dragons, Nintendo and Other Occult Adventures

Moreover ye see and hear, that not alone at Ephesus, but almost throughout all Asia, this Paul hath persuaded and turned away much people, saying that there be no gods which are made with hands. (Acts 19:26)

In one TV ad for kids, a tribe of blue savages worships a talking Pee Wee doll, chanting. (USA Today, October 26, 1988)

The New Age has conspired to use the toy industry to seduce our children and to undermine an entire generation's trust in God. I make this statement boldly and without reservation. If you are not disturbed about the New Age occult intervention into our kids' minds through hideous toys and games, you need to get on your knees now, this moment, and ask God for discernment and ask Him to place on your heart a burden for kids' souls. Please! The need is desperate.

Toy after toy is designed to introduce young children's minds to New Age and occult ideas and symbols. Such toys include dolls and paraphernalia of *He-Man* and *She-Ra*, licensed cartoon characters that are depicted as possessing occultic, superhuman powers. Some toys are *exact representations of demons*--for example, action figures originating from the TV series *Black Star*. The *Black Star* toy demon figurines actually glow in the dark. The *Masters of the Universe* series offers toy figures of occult personalities named *Ram Man* and *Beast Man*. Also available for children: stickers depicting occult creatures and New Age and Satanic symbols, robot mechanical toys that represent the dark forces of evil, and a wide selection of toys that are emblazoned with New Age Satanic symbols. These include a skateboard with dragons and other grotesque markings.

Meanwhile, popular fantasy games created for children embody Satanic symbols and instill occult and esoteric teachings into the minds of the young. Such role playing games include the infamous *Dungeons & Dragons; Photon*, a mind-warping space-age entertainment game; Nintendo's *Wizards & Warriors* video game; and *Assassin*, a game in which players put out "contracts" on each other's lives. These role playing games assign children such roles as deities, demigods, and demons and give instructions on casting spells and using magic circles, Satanic pentagrams, and occultic triangles.

Also popular with kids are card and board games with explicit Satanic and New Age themes, such as tarot cards, runes, and the ouija board. Our ministry continues to receive letters revealing true case stories of young people who become demon-possessed and whose minds became confused, demented, and psychotic after exposure to these occultic-oriented games.

Below, we will examine just a few of the thousands of action toys, dolls, and fantasy games now on the market. According to the Toy Manufacturers of America Association, 8.2 billion--*that's billion*--dollars was spent last year by American parents and kids for toys. This does not include the hundreds of millions spent for games. Not every toy or game is evil. Praise God, some good and wholesome secular toys and even some outstanding Christian toys and games are now being produced. We need them. But on the whole, Satan has an eight billion dollar-plus industry devoted entirely to him in the manufacture of toys.

"Cries and Screams Are Music to My Ears!"

"Soundwave" is one of the toys that Satan must be especially pleased with. Kids love Soundwave because he's unrelentingly evil. A mechanical robot toy in the shape of a cassette recorder, Soundwave surprises as he unfolds into a terror robot whose motto, the manufacturer says, is "Cries and screams are music to my ears."

The ancient Babylonian fire god, Moloch (also worshiped in another name by the Druids and Egyptians), was undoubtedly the model for this toy. Moloch was a hideous god smeared with the blood of human sacrifices. As parents approached the giant stone image of Moloch and sacrificed their children to his raging fires, an orchestra of musicians played loudly on drums and timbrels. This drowned out the cries and screams of the children being sacrificed to the grim idol.

Alexander Hislop, in *The Two Babylons*, said of Moloch:

Human victims were his most acceptable offerings; human groans and wailings were the sweetest music in his ears; human tortures were believed to delight his heart.[1]

Are we, today, sacrificing the very souls of our children to Moloch, by allowing them to worship his image in the form of a toy idol?

Nintendo's WIZARDS & WARRIORS is similar to DUNGEONS & DRAGONS in its occultism.

Sorcery and the Occult in Video: Nintendo's "Wizards & Warriors" and More

Nintendo's interactive video entertainment system is the hottest toy on the market today. "Is there anything wrong with Nintendo?" parents constantly ask our ministry.

Again, parental discretion is vital. Nintendo could potentially be a good toy for kids, but the makers, in their greed for sales, have injected into Nintendo the sorcery and occultism that seem so popular with kids today. One example is the Nintendo video game *Wizards & Warriors* in which "Kuros, the knight warrior" heroically battles the evil wizard, Malkil. The problem is that the good guy, Kuros, also avails himself of magic and sorcery to win in his struggles, meaning that kids playing this game should do likewise in overcoming the obstacles in their own lives.

Nintendo's *Wizards & Warriors* is permeated with scenes of dungeons, levitation, mysterious potions, demonic warriors who can fly and crawl ("the undead"), magical swords of light and so on.

And Now for Your Kids: The Dread Black Horse of Revelation 6!

A few years ago, when my wife, Wanda, and I read Phil Phillips' outstanding expose' of Satanism in kids' toys, *Turmoil in the Toy Box*,[2] our spirits were troubled. Since Phil wrote that book, what changes, if any, have been made on the toy scene? A recent trip to just one *Toys R Us* store provided the answer: toys have not improved. Today they're even more sinister and dangerous to our children.

We found an entire assortment of "Official Advanced Dungeons & Dragons" action toys. One, however, stands out as especially horrendous. Black in color, it's called the "Evil Nightmare Flying Horse-like Creature." On the outer package of this made-in-hell toy is the following description:

> *Evil Nightmare!* An evil horse-like creature kept alive by black magic, the "Nightmare" is the sinister mount of Warduke, Evil Fighter and other evil characters. What makes a "Nightmare" even more dangerous is that it can fly and attack enemies without a rider to command it. The "Nightmare" uses its razor fangs, flaming hooves, and smoking, fog-like breath as weapons during battle.

The Bible gives us a chilling description of what this nightmarish toy represents. In Revelation 6, we learn of the four horses of the apocalypse. They will bring death, hell, destruction, and bloodshed to planet earth in the coming Great Tribulation period. Their hellish master is Lucifer. The *black horse* is one of the four: "And when he had opened the third seal, I heard the third beast say, come and see and I beheld, and lo, a black horse. . ." (Rev. 6:5).

Evil Nightmare Flying Horse-like Creature

Skeletor and His Ram's Head Scepter

Another loathsome and demonic action toy encountered was *Skeletor*, manufactured by Mattel. Skeletor is part of the "Masters of the Universe" collection. The instruction sheet for this dark toy of evil informs the child who becomes its owner:

> When you put on your Skeletor helmet and armored belt you become transformed into an agent of evil. Use your power sword shield to combat good. With your mystical

ram's head scepter you will be able to call forth the denizens of darkness to help conquer the forces of good.

Dark Dragon, Evil Battle Beast and the Inhumanoids

Among other toys Wanda and I discovered on our toy-hunting expedition--that *one trip* to a toy store--were the following:

Dark Dragon, Evil Battle Beast. This is a menacing red and black (Satanic colors) flying dragon with teeth bared. It supposedly uses its hologram powers to do evil.

The Inhumanoids. Their eyes glow in the dark. They are rotten tree trunks that spring to life as monsters. The attraction for the kids is that these are collapsible toys. They look harmless but when extended become monstrous. The package touts this feature as "The Evil that Lies Within."

Skateboard Rides to Hades

Some skateboards we have seen were covered with decals and drawings of skulls, bones, fiery dragons, Satanic symbols, and even gruesome dead human bodies.

Myths, Monsters, and Masks

Toy stores of the *Toys R Us* chain are not the only stores pushing these toys. The disease infecting kids' toys and games is everywhere. Here are some of the items we've since found available elsewhere:

Myths and Monsters Card Game for Your Birthday. This card game for birthday parties includes cards of all the gods, goddesses, and beasts of ancient mythologies, from the pegasus and centaur to Zeus, Jupiter, Neptune, and Hercules. The package reads:

Gods and goddesses, monsters and myths.
The wicked Medusa, too--
This Game should be exciting for someone smart as you.

More Masks to Color, Cut Out, and Wear. Kids can make-believe they are pirates, clowns, and lions. They can also pretend to be the Mother Goddess with a star on her forehead, or any one of a number of devils, including the horned goat god. All they have to do is color, cut out and wear the masks found in this book.

Crystar, Crystal Warrior. This is an activity book series, allowing the kids to color and work puzzles, games, and mazes. It includes exciting action scenes of Crystar, the Crystal Warrior, whose overlord (supposedly "good") is the vile-faced wizard Ogeode. You will find sorcery and wizardry, crystals, disguised Satanic symbols, and sexy women in these activity books.

Ogeode is the "good" wizard who uses his sorcery powers to create crystal warriors.

*This mask of the unicorn ram's head and other satanic masks
were offered to kids in the activity book to color,
cut-out and wear.*

The Leather Goddesses and the Mark

Parents whose kids enjoy whizzing away on the home
computer with software games should also closely examine these games. Every abomination imaginable is now
offered by software companies. Recently, in newspapers
across the nation, Waldenbooks, the huge bookstore
chain, advertised a number of computer software games
as "gifts" for kids. Two caught my eye: *Trilogy: Three
Mind Stretching Adventures* and *Leather Goddesses of
Phobos.* The cover of *Trilogy* showed a gruesome hand
with the Mark of Satan--in this instance, the pentagram--
carved on it!

"Dungeons & Dragons" and "Dragonraid"

The ever-popular *Dungeons & Dragons* fantasy role-playing game is ever-present in toy stores and department stores. This game is nothing more than an introduction to the occult. Fantasies the players involve and indulge themselves in include murder, rape, arson, pillage, terrorism, brutal torture, etc. Kids also take on the names of actual demons.

Dragonraid was designed for kids as a "Christian" substitute for *Dungeons & Dragons (D&D)*. The manufacturer has got to be kidding! This is *worse* than *D&D* because it presents to the child *evil* disguised in the form of *good*. It is a blasphemous thing to paint evil as good. *Dragonraid* is a prime example of how Satanic deception is infiltrating the Christian community.

Two esoteric fantasy posters sold by the *Dragonraid* company to promote their Satanic game should suffice to point out the inherent New Age occultic overtones. One depicts a beautiful medieval princess in a flowing white dress (the goddess) leading a white charger through a meadow. The double moon and an etheric castle beckon beyond in the sky. The Bible quote that serves as the caption is John 8:32: "You will know the truth, and the truth shall make you free."

A second poster, called "Lightraider with Unicorn," shows us a medieval damsel in a meadow, hand outstretched toward a feisty white unicorn horse that has an unusually long, pointed single horn protruding from between its eyes. The caption reads, "The Lord will rescue me from every evil attack and will bring me safely to His heavenly kingdom. To Him be glory for ever and ever. Amen (2 Timothy 4:18)."

The unicorn has the "little horn" of the beast mentioned by the prophet Daniel in his prophetic book of the Bible. It does *not* have any relationship to God but is a symbol of Satan. The unicorn's roots lie in pagan idolatry. Any student of paganism will quickly discover this indisputable fact. Occultism embraces the unicorn as symbolic of *its god*:

> Unicorn is a god. He demands servitude and sacrifice. He stands out of reach, as fixed and brilliant as the stars.
> Hail, Unicorn! God of knowledge; a dark ghost on the fringes of man's consciousness. . . .
> The unicorn stands alone, still as frost. It keeps watch down corridors of time. The past and the future meet in the presence of the unicorn: the darkness and light become one.[3]

The Road to Disaster

The sad and frightening fact is that many of today's toys and games are constant reminders of the power of Satan's New Age occultists to worm their way into every aspect of our kids' lives. Our kids are traveling down the yellow brick road to disaster. Society is breeding an entire generation of monsters. It is no wonder, then, that in the '60's, kids tripped out on drugs, but today our kids are tripping out on Satanism. That's the regrettable subject of the chapter that follows.

THIRTEEN

Teens Trip Out on Satan: The Rise of Hard-Core Devil Worship and Witchcraft Among Our Youth

Yea, they sacrificed their sons and daughters unto devils. And shed innocent blood, even the blood of their sons and daughters, whom they sacrificed unto the idols . . . and the land was polluted with blood. Thus they were defiled with their own works, and went a whoring with their own inventions. Therefore was the wrath of the Lord kindled. . . .

(Psalm 106:37-40)

Dr. Al Carlisle, Utah State Prison System, estimated that between 40,000 and 60,000 ritual Satanic homicides per year occur in the United States. Dr. Carlisle based this estimate upon the number of Satan worshippers. . . . Ritual murders in Satanic worship generally involve mutilation, mayhem and sexual assault culminating in the heart being cut out of the victim strapped to an alter.

(Lt. Larry Jones,
Police Investigator)

S ay you love Satan!" Ricky yelled. "Go on." The knife slashed warm flesh for the third time.

"Say it! Say you love Satan!"

"No!" Gary screamed in Pain. "No!"

"Say it, . . . " Ricky demanded. "I'm gonna keep it up until you do! Say you love Satan!"

"No!" Gary yelled, and tried to roll away from the unerring blade. "I love my mother! I don't love Satan! I love my mother!"

"Satan!" Ricky hollered, and the knife blade found its mark again. "I won't stop until you say you love Satan!"

"My mother," Gary cried, "I love my mother!"

Ricky, knife still in his hand, began to babble and in a terrible frenzy started stabbing Gary's face. The knife blade plunged into the eye sockets. . . . He slashed at the nose and the mouth, wildly plunging the blade over and over again until Gary's body was flat on the ground once more and his terrible fright had passed.

Ricky and Jimmy stood by the fire, looking at each other. Overhead a crow cawed, then circled lazily. Even though the sky was pitch black, both boys could make out the bird's form as it flew and squawked above them.

"Satan's with us," Ricky said. "That crow is a sign. Satan approves of what we have done in his name."

"You better get yourself cleaned up," Jimmy said. "You can't let people see you like that, all bloody."

"I did it, man." Ricky grinned. "I made my first sacrifice, my first sacrifice for Satan." [1]

* * * *

The phone rang in the Northpoint Police Station. It was about 2:30 a.m.

"I want to report a disturbance," a woman's voice said.

"What kind of a disturbance, ma'am?" the officer asked.

"There has been screaming and there is a fire and they're playing loud music. It woke me and my husband up."

"Where is this?" asked the cop.

"We live in Woodhull Place. The noise is above us in the woods."

"Astakea Woods?"

"Sorry, ma'am, but that's private property up there."

"So what? It's two-thirty in the morning! We can't sleep!"

"Private property, ma'am. Can't go up there without a warrant."

"But it woke us up."

"Probably just a bunch of kids, ma'am. They'll get tired after awhile. They'll stop soon."

"But we heard screaming."

"You know how kids are, ma'am."

"But we heard screaming."

"You know how kids are, ma'am."

"But suppose something's happened up there?"

"Private property, ma'am."

"But. . . ."

"Go back to sleep, ma'am."[2]

* * * *

"Go back to sleep." That's what the world and Satan would have us do today. Even as our children and teen-agers are being ravaged and scarred by the darkest, most violent outpouring of New Age occultism ever to hit the face of this globe, alarmed parents are soothingly being lulled into a state of apathy. "Nothing to worry about, ma'am. Everything's O.K. Go back to sleep."

That's exactly what concerned callers who rang up the Northpoint, Long Island police station were told: that all was well, probably just the shenanigans normally to be attributed to kids. But the awful truth was far different. In a small, forest-like clump of trees and shrubbery lay a dead seventeen-year-old, Gary Lauwer. His teen attack-ers had brutally savaged and murdered the young high schooler because he had failed to pay up for illegal drugs bought.

It was a case that shocked and rocked the tiny Long Island community of Northpoint, which lies just outside of the teeming metropolis of New York City. Three teens who had dabbled in the occult and had conducted rituals to Satan had grown more and more weird and evil as they filled their thoughts with the wild, blasphemous sounds of heavy metal rock groups like Ozzy Osbourne of Black Sabbath.

Too, their minds had become dimmed through drug and alcohol abuse. All told, the dark combination of occultism, Satanic rock music and drugs had proven fatal, both for the three young attackers . . . and for their tragic victim, Gary Lauwer.

The Explosion of New Age Satanism and Occultism Among Our Youth

The explosion of occultism among our youth should not come as a surprise to Christians. Years ago, New Age and occult leaders worked out detailed and precise plans for bringing the souls of our youth into captivity to Satan. For several decades now, New Age teachers and gurus have been indoctrinating our kids, steadily introducing their susceptible minds and tender hearts to crude, sadistic doctrines of demons.

The horror that befell Gary Lauwer on that fatal day in Northpoint was only one by-product of the malevolent doctrines now embraced by millions of influential adults and constantly being imparted to our kids. Christians who love children can only cry when they see the damage being done in the name of the New Age.

Our Holy Bible prophesied that in the last days this would be so. Paul warned:

> Now the spirit speaketh expressly that in the latter time
> some shall depart from the faith, giving heed to seducing
> spirits and doctrines of devils (1 Tim. 4:1, 2).

Across the United States of America, in Canada,
Australia, Great Britain and on the European
continent--indeed, throughout the world today--we are
seeing the bitter harvest of the decades-long spreading of
these doctrines of demons by New Age teachers. A tidal
wave of witchcraft, Satanism and other blackish forms of
occultism are sweeping our nations.

"Three years ago, nobody wanted to hear it, nobody
believed it was real," San Francisco police detective
Sandi Gallant told an Associated Press reporter. Yet
today, evidence is mounting of human and animal sacrifices by Satanists and witches. Sexual molestation and
torture of young children is also being reported. The
New Age religion is behind this dark and malicious occult
revival. Yet, few in the secular media care to report on
this connection. For example, who in the TV and print
news media have reported that thousands of copies of the
revealing book *Occult Preparations for a New Age*, have
recently been sold through New Age and occult bookstores?

Incredibly, television and radio talk show hosts are
aiding and abetting the Satanism explosion. Witches and
spirit channelers are regular guests on shows as varied as
"Larry King Live," "Good Morning America," and "Phil
Donahue." Michael Aquino, self-styled High Priest of
Satan for San Francisco's Temple of Set, appeared on the
popular "Oprah Winfrey Show."

Meanwhile, police in cities and towns in almost every
state in the U.S.A. are bewildered and confused. They
have received little or no training in how to combat the
wicked criminal activities of Satanic groups and
witchcraft covens.

Our father which art in Hell,
hallowed be thy name. Thy Kingdom
is come, Thy will be done; On earth
As it in Hell!

We take this night our rightful
due, And trespass not on paths of
pain. Lead us unto temptation, And
deliver us from false piety, for
Thine is the Kingdom And the power
And the glory forever!

And let reason rule the earth.

Deliver us, O Mighty Satan, from
all past error And delusion, that, having set our foot upon the path of darkness And vowed ourselves to Thy services, We may not weaken in our resolve,
but with Thy assistance, grow in
wisdom And strength.

Shemhamforash! Hail Satan!

*At the top of this page is the cover of THE SATANIC BIBLE
by Anton LaVey. Above is a prayer to Satan found by police on
the possession of a teenager.
On the following page is The Nine Satanic
Statements which LaVey claims to be official doctrine
of the Church of Satan.*

THE
NINE
SATANIC
STATEMENTS

1   Satan represents indulgence, instead of abstinence!

2   Satan represents vital existence, instead of spiritual
pipe dreams!

3   Satan represents undefiled wisdom, instead of
hypocritical self-deceit!

4   Satan represents kindness to those who deserve it,
instead of love wasted on ingrates!

5   Satan represents vengeance, instead of turning
the other cheek!

6   Satan represents responsibility to the responsible,
instead of concern for psychic vampires!

7   Satan represents man as just another animal,
sometimes better, more often worse than those that
walk on all-fours, who, because of his "divine spiritual
and intellectual development," has become the
most vicious animal of all!

8   Satan represents all of the so-called sins, as they
all lead to physical, mental, or emotional gratification!

9   Satan has been the best friend the church has ever had,
as he has kept it in business all these years!

Anton Szandor LaVey

Symbols of Satan.
Top Row from left to right: the "peace sign," the pentagram in the form of an amulet, and the point within the circle, indicating Lucifer as the point of light inside the sun. Bottom Row from left to right: the sign of anarchy, the pentagram with the two horns pointing up, and the triangle (pointing up or down), the sign of the unholy trinity.

Actual art drawing submitted by a fourth grader as a school project.

HAIL SATANAS!

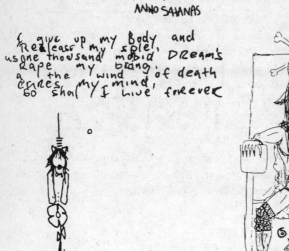

I GET MY SATANIC BIBLE BACK
11/12/85
ANNO SATANAS

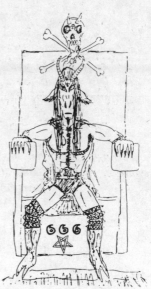

Occult drawings confiscated by police officer from teens involved in Satanism.

Teenagers involved in Satanism often use magic formulas, symbols, markings, and designs similar to the above and found in various occult books.

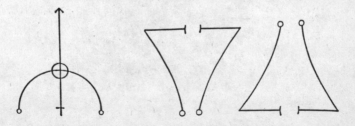

Trail markers indicate locations where activities of Satanic covens or groups will take place. These are only three of many trail marker signs in use.

More symbols of evil: left, the "cross of confusion" questions the validity of Christianity. 666 is the number of the beast and the letter F is the sixth number in the alphabet.

Occult symbols on clothing such as this jean jacket have become the rage among teens. Note the all-seeing eye (the Sun God) and the infinity 8 sign (Lucifer shall reign for eternity).

The New Age movement is merely hard-core Satanism with a thin veneer of intellectualism, glamor and glitter to lend respectability. The New Age doesn't praise "Satan" but instead honors the *Force* (who is Satan). New Agers don't communicate and take orders from demons but instead they follow instructions from their *Spirit Guides* (who are demons). The New Age is Satanism prettied up. It is Satan and his hosts of dark angels disguised as "angels of light" (II Cor. 11:14).

Music From the Pit

One of the greatest contributors to the occult devastation among our youth is music. Satan principally has two types of dark music he is using to subvert and possess youth: heavy metal rock and New Age "mood" music.

I have yet to learn of one youth heavily involved in Satanism who is not also a hardened addict and fan of heavy metal music. This music is born in hell and raised up to destroy and maul the mind. The lyrics of the more popular hits by the occult recording artists of heavy metal amply demonstrate that this is music that praises Lucifer. These are hymns to the devil.

For example, the group *Merciful Fate* performs these lyrics in its song, "The Oath:"

By the Symbol of the Creator, I swear henceforth to be
A faithful Servant of his most puissant Arch-Angel
The Prince Lucifer
Whom the Creator designated as His Regent
And Lord of this World. Amen.
I deny Jesus Christ, the Deceiver
And I adjure the Christian Faith
Holding in Contempt all of its Works.
Solo: M.D. Solo: H.S.

As a being now possessed of a human
Body in this World I swear to give my full
    allegiance
To its lawful Master, to worship
Him Our Lord Satan, and no other
In the name of Satan, the ruler of Earth
Open wide the Gates of Hell and come
Forth from the Abyss
By these Names: Satan, Leviathan,
Belial, Lucifer
I will kiss the Goat.
Solo: M.D. Solo: H.S.

I swear to give my Mind, my Body and Soul
    unreservedly
To the furtherance of our Lord Satan's
    Designs
Do What Thou Wilt, Shall Be The Whole
    Of the Law
As it was in the Beginning, is now, and
    ever shall be
World Without End, Amen.
Solo: H.S. - M.D.

The Hidden Dangers of New Age Music

New Age music--called "mood," "contemplative," "medi-tative," etc.--is even more deadly to the spirit than heavy metal rock. Most New Age music is instrumental, so the question inevitably arises: how can *instrumental music* be harmful? Those who ask this question simply do not understand the effects of music. Any music expert will tell you that the beat, tone, cadence, and arrangement of music is the key to affecting human moods. Lyrics, or words, play only a minimal role. Instrumental music can make you feel blue, moody and depressed or zippy, peppy, and upbeat. It can inspire you or drag you down.
    Instrumental music can invite in demons--as sorcer-ers, shamans and witchdoctors well know--or drive them

away. God's instrumental music, played on a harp by David, put demons to flight:

> And it came to pass, when the evil spirit from God was upon Saul, that David took a harp, and played with his hand: so Saul was refreshed, and was well, and the evil spirit departed from him. (1 Sam. 16:23)

New Age music, on the other hand, is designed by the best musician in the world to conjure up and invite demons into the listener's mind. The magical genius of Lucifer, its composer, far exceeds that of Mozart, Beethoven, Wagner, and all the other great composers who have ever lived. The Bible tells us that *Lucifer was originally designed by God as a living, thinking, musical instrument* (see Ezek. 28:13). Satan knows how to make New Age music that can conquer man's mind.

Satan has also trained up demon specialists in music who give music to their human followers that has been readied in advance in hell. Some of the people who produce New Age music are not aware that demon spirits are secretly implanting this music in their minds. But many *are* aware and approve.

One particular demon named Koothoomi (also spelled "Kuthumi"), has reportedly appeared to a number of New Agers and given them music packaged in the pit. Here's how one New Age musician described a visitation by his hypnotic demon music instructor:

> From far away I heard the strains of an organ with which was mingled the sound of voices so pure and ethereal as to suggest the chanting of a celestial choir. . . . The music was unlike any music I had heard before. It was subtle, yet melodious, sweet, yet devoid of all sentimental lusciousness; at one moment powerful and awe-awakening, at another soft and tender as the caress of an angel's hand. It was my brother Koothoomi playing on the pipes.

Suddenly, a voice spoke out, "Listen well, and remember for one day you shall give such music to the world."[3]

New Age music is designed to bring the listener into a peaceful and hypnotic trance state during which demons can easily enter and take possession. It's been called "electronic meditation."[4] A number of the New Age instrumentals have hidden *subliminal messages*. Supposedly, these messages can reprogram or rescript your brain. As one of the best known New Age composers and musicians, Brother Charles, recently told *Meditation* magazine:

> I can open the doors of your (brain's) databanks. . . .
> As you're listening, the rescripting process is happening automatically via subliminally recorded messages.[5]

The dangers are clear. New Age music--instrumental music--is composed by demons who are trained and empowered by their Master to use this music to possess men's bodies. Subliminal messages imbedded in the music aid in this objective. New Age music can easily overwhelm the senses of young people and adults alike. Because it is more subtle and deceptive, it is even more harmful and deadly than any other form of music, including heavy metal.

Self-Styled Satanists

From police reports and the results of extensive investigation, it has become known that there are two types of Satanists and devil worshipers: *self-styled* and *organized networks*. The first, the self-styled Satanist, is by far the most prevalent. This teenager or adult develops a fascination or an obsession with the occult by watching occult-oriented movies, reading magical fantasy novels, esoteric science fiction novels, and studying manuals and guides on Egyptian and Celtic magic, witchcraft and Satanism now readily available at libraries and bookstores.

The self-styled young Satanist may also learn all he knows about Satanism from his advanced peers or from adults who practice the occult arts. The occult symbols, phrases, and behaviors exhibited on MTV rock videos are also of use to the self-styled Satanist as are the lessons learned from the new breed of occult comic books, and the occultism found in *Dungeons & Dragons* and other fantasy role playing games.

Most kids involved today in devil worship, Satanism, and witchcraft fall into this category. But as they join together and assemble into covens, they often get caught up in higher stakes organizations controlled by adults.

Networks of Devil Worshipers

There are a number of Satanic organizations and groups which are today networking together. They recruit young people into their ranks but only after careful deliberations. The twisted leaders of these groups are the masterminds who run kidnapping rings and torture mills, author occultic books and collude together to promote Satan's agenda for the last days. Most operate behind closed doors and their membership is kept secret.

Their networking collusion is in person and by computer networking. According to Jack Roper, a Christian researcher who is one of the nation's top experts on the occult, the national and international computer networks that link these people include the Baphonet-Baphonet Network, Thelemante, Tahutinet, Athexaea Camp, Weirdbase, Golden Dawn, Crescent Moon, and Pagan BBS.[6]

Satanism Among the Very Young

Reports pouring into our ministry show that the devil worshiping phenomenon extends down to the youngest of kids. In Austin, Texas a mother told of her young seven-year-old son who had become an MTV (rock video) addict. One Sunday morning as the family prepared for church, suddenly her son blurted out, "Mom, I don't want to go. I don't like Jesus. Lucifer is my God."

Jack Roper, whose organization, C.A.R.I.S. (Christian Apologetics Research and Information Service), monitors and traces Satanic activity among teens and kids recently sent me a two-inch stack of newspaper and other clippings from around the country. Kids as young as six, seven, and eight are into Satanic graffiti, occult dress, heavy metal "black" rock music, and sexual perversions caused by involvement in Satanic activities. Meanwhile, adult Satanists and witches prepare kids two to four years old for later use in evil rituals.

Teen crime occurring as a result of Satanism is at an all-time high. Thousands of animal sacrifices, sex orgies, the drinking of human and animal blood, vandalism, robberies, and rapes can be attributed to teenage devil worship, witchcraft covens and self-styled Satanists who form into roving gangs. Telephone utility boxes, buses, trains, subways, fences, buildings, and sides of houses in many cities and towns are regularly marred and defaced by teens involved in Satanism. School teachers report that the most popular topics for theme and term papers by teenagers involve the occult and Satanism.

Newspapers Tell the Grim Story

Among the criminal acts committed by teenage devil worshippers in the past year alone were the following:

Mendocino County, California. Children were raped at a preschool while being forced to chant, "Baby Jesus is dead."

Cresson, Pennsylvania. Teenagers reportedly over-turned tombstones in cemeteries, spray-painted Satanic symbols and graffiti and the number 666 around town, killed and nailed a cat to a tree, and sacrificed a rabbit by tearing its heart out while the animal was alive and drinking its blood. The young man who was the leader of the Satanic group later shot and killed himself.

Beckville, Texas. High school seniors threw a drinking party and showed the film, *The Faces of Death*, a so-called "snuff" movie in which people are actually tortured and murdered while the vile acts are being filmed. The fatal result was that one of the youth's then invited a blind girl who was attending the party outside, abducted her, took her to a cemetery, and strangled and bludgeoned her. Then, he returned to the house where the party was going on with blood all over his arms and shirt. The kids at the party calmly helped the youth clean up and did not report the murder to the police.

Houston, Texas. A young man named Amos Edward Smith participated in six ritualistic killings in which the victims, including an infant, were decapitated, dismembered or mutilated and had their throats cut. The young man, now on death row in the Texas State Prison at Huntsville, told investigators he and others sacrificed the victims to voodoo gods, so the gods would empower them to get things they wanted but couldn't pay for.

Dallas, Texas. Young girls, from 11 to 14-years-old, told police officers about Satanic rituals in which men gave them alcohol and drugs, read from a Satanic bible, and forced them to participate in bizarre sex acts. Physical exams substantiated the story.

Denver, Colorado. The mother and father of a 16-year-old suicide victim found their dead son barefoot with ritual symbols drawn on the ground around his body. In search of an explanation, they went to his room and found $150 worth of paperback books on Satanic rituals, candles, incense, powders, Dungeons & Dragons books, heavy metal rock albums, occult magazines, a wall hanging of an inverted pentagram, and a knife collection. The youth's school notebook, decorated with a unicorn, was filled with Satanic drawings and writings. The parents explained to authorities that they knew little about what their son was doing as far as Satanic activity was concerned. "There's a big push today," said the mother, "to build trust with kids. So we tried to give him his privacy." She said she knew he sometimes took drugs such as acid (LSD) and hashish but thought that it wasn't a real problem.

Parents and Satanism

Grievous damage is done to children today because of the attitude expressed above. Pop psychologists are telling parents, "give your kids space," let them have their privacy, demonstrate trust. . . ." God's prescription for parenting success--His guide to raising children is far different. Yes, God wants us to be loving, kind, and considerate to our children--we are not to exasperate children or provoke them to anger. But we are to set clear guidelines and rules of behavior. Love is *not* permissiveness. Moreover, if Satanism is not to gain access into the lives of their children, *parents must be parents*.

Parents who truly care must know what their kids are into--and up to. And when the child goes across that fine line of acceptable behavior, Mom and Dad must put their collective feet down. To say you love your children, then, through permissiveness--to allow your children to go to hell, literally. This is not love, it is not trust nor respect. It is insanity.

What to Do if You Suspect Your Child is Involved in Satanism

You can know if your child is involved in Satanic activity, and you can take positive steps to help your child overcome the Satanic and occultic influences in his or her life. If you suspect your child--or a child you are concerned about--is involved in Satan, please be sure to read Chapter 14, especially the sections entitled "20 Warning Signs of Satanism" and "Seven Steps to Overcoming Occultism and Satanic Involvement."

FOURTEEN

Victory in Jesus! What Must Christian Parents Do?

Submit yourselves therefore to God. Resist the Devil and he will flee from you. (James 4:7)

Wherefore God also hath highly exalted Him and given Him a name which is above every name: That at the name of Jesus every knee should bow, of things in heaven, and things in earth, and things under the earth; and that every tongue should confess that Jesus Christ is Lord, to the glory of God the Father. (Philippians 2:9-11)

It is undeniable that Satan has a Master Plan to seize absolute control of Planet Earth and its people. Our children are a primary target of this evil plan; indeed the Lord of Hell has made the winning of our children's souls a top priority. So determined are Satan and his New Age disciples to capture our youth that they do not intend to let you or I, as Christians, interfere or prevent this mean-spirited goal from being attained.

How can we successfully thwart Satan's Plan and pluck our children from the coming fire? With God, all things are possible, including this. We *must* totally depend on God and His divine protection and we *can* know that He is able.

Call on God . . . He is Able

The real key to safeguarding our children is to avail ourselves of the incomparable powers of God. Yes, I am convinced that as parents, grandparents, and concerned Christians, there are things we can do ourselves, but only with the help of God. We should be activists in this world, obeying its laws, yet obedient to a superior law-- that of God. There are criminal laws on the books designed to protect children from the pornography we see so prevalent in everything from movies to comic books. We should work to see that they are enforced and seek tougher laws. There are civil laws, state and national, that prohibit the teaching of Eastern religions-- indeed, any religion--when that teaching is intended to put down and subjugate Christianity. We need to become aware of these statutes and insist on our rights.

As long as we have remaining any semblance of democratic free rights, we must insist that the government protect our children and render fair and equal treatment in schools and elsewhere for them. And we must band together as Christians so we will have the strength of numbers. If, for example, corporate advertisers of some of TV's worst and most offensive programs for children discover that Christian parents will not buy their products, they may well decide to reconsider where their advertising dollars go.

Arm Ourselves With Knowledge

Another important thing we must do as concerned Christians who love our children is arm ourselves with *knowledge.* Reading this book and other excellent books exposing the New Age threat will keep you abreast of what the leaders of the New Age religion plan to do to our kids. Three books I particularly recommend are *Hidden Dangers of the Rainbow* by Constance Cumbey; *Peace, Prosperity and the Coming Holocaust*, by Dave Hunt, and *The Lucifer Connection*, by Joseph Carr.

However, I beg you, be wary! Already a number of supposedly anti-New Age books are coming into the market which are, upon examination, *books written by those who wish to compromise the Gospel.*

For example, in the book *Understanding the New Age*, author Russell Chandler, a *Los Angeles Times* reporter, claims that the New Age isn't all *that* bad. It's not all "chaff," he insists, there's "wheat" there, too. The Bible warns us against such evil doctrines. We cannot drink from the same cup as devils. We are to have *no part* in the works of darkness, but rather we are to reprove and expose them (Eph. 5:11).

Jesus did not seek compromise with the Pharisees, Moses did not "cut a deal" with Pharaoh, and Paul did not preach regarding the Roman and Greek mystery religions of his day that there was "wheat" in those pagan religions. So let us contend for the *undefiled faith*, not wavering, not growing weary.

In the coming months, there will be many who advise us to compromise with the New Age, to "dialogue" and "seek common ground." We who refuse to bend our wills to this Antichrist monster religion will be branded as narrow, unloving, divisive, and separative. Our response should be, *Praise God!* Jesus, too, was characterized as unloving, narrow, divisive, and separative. Should we who choose to be His servants expect any better treatment from the world than Jesus received? Even the "world" inside the Church?

If the world hate you, ye know that it hated Me before it hated you. If ye were of the world, the world would love his own: but because ye are not of the world, but I have chosen you out of the world, therefore, the world hateth you.

(John 15:18, 19)

For consider Him that endured such contradiction of sinners against Himself, lest ye be wearied and faint in your minds. (Heb. 12:3)

Let us then say *no* to the New Age. Let us say *yes* to our Lord Jesus Christ. Without reservation and without compromise.

Read and Trust in God's Word

I pray that this book has been a blessing to you. God called me to write it, and I know He wants you to be informed and knowledgeable of these things. But always, we must keep our eyes fixed on Jesus and His Word. Yes, we are to expose the New Age darkness. Indeed, God commands us to do so. But our priority must be Jesus. My own rule of thumb is: *Major on Jesus, minor on the devil.*

There is no substitute for God's Word, either. My book, or any other book, is a pale substitute. In fact, it's not a substitute at all. If we are to successfully challenge the New Age assault on our kids, only the Word of God, the Bible, will provide us with the means to do so. Let us praise our Lord that He has provided us with His magnificent Word.

The word of God is quick, and powerful, and sharper than any two-edged sword, piercing even to the dividing asunder of soul and spirit, and of joints and marrow, and is a discerner of the thoughts and intents of the heart.

(Hebrews 4:12)

Witness to Others

It is our privilege and our responsibility to contend for the faith and to witness to all of the Love and Truth of our Lord Jesus Christ.

No doubt most will reject your message of Truth. They will continue in their rebellion against God and His Son. Some, in their effort to steal your children, will even attempt to seduce you--to turn you away from God and toward the lies of the New Age religion:

> Whosoever denieth the Son, the same hath not the Father: but he that acknowledgeth the Son hath the Father also. . . . These things have I written concerning them that seduce you. (I John 2:23, 26)

Persevere, but do not despair when people reject your message of Love and Salvation. Rejoice even when they revile and persecute you (see John 15:18-19; 15:25; 16:2), for in so doing you will receive a blessing from the Lord (Matt. 5:10-11).

A Simple Message is Often Best

A simple message is often the best when witnessing. Sometimes you can argue with an unsaved person for hours over a particular New Age teaching or practice. You can talk until you are blue in the face but you may never convince that person you are right. Remember, though, that while your own words of argument and persuasion may be of little value, the *Word of God does not return void* (Isaiah 55:11). It always hits the mark even when there is no immediate response. Preach the Word and let the Holy Spirit convict.

To truly help a New Ager, appraise that person of John 3:7: "Ye must be born again." Bring him or her to a knowledge of Ephesians 2:8, 9: "For by grace are ye saved through faith; and that not of yourselves: it is the gift of God." And most important, testify of John 3:16: "For God so loved the world that He gave His only begotten Son that whosoever believeth in Him should not perish, but have eternal life." Eternal life, only through Jesus Christ, the real Jesus, the Word who was God and is God forevermore (John 1).

Give Thanks

In all things give thanks to God, especially for His protection of our children. God's power is sufficient even in a world where evil abounds. He answers the prayers of His people for He loves us. Believe this and you will never fail.

Our Attitude Toward Our Children

As I have emphasized throughout this book, God has laid upon each of us the burden and the responsibility--and the joy--of raising our children to become men and women of God. We do this through firmness and resolute discipline mixed with love, understanding, and tenderness (see Eph. 6:4).

Children also have a responsibility. One of the Ten Commandments is to honor one's parents. Paul further instructs children: "Children, *obey* your parents in the Lord, for this is right" (Eph. 6:1). In Jude, we also read that we are not to despise those who have dominion over us.

Our children must be taught that the ways of their peers and the ways of the world are often not the ways of wisdom. They must recognize that the strong, upright person does not primarily seek approval from peers, but from God.

Finally, our children should be encouraged to participate *with us* in spiritual warfare. Kids can be great little warriors who witness to their friends at school and to neighbor kids about the dangers of the New Age. So inspire your children in this direction.

What to Do if Your Child Becomes Involved in the New Age

It is always tragic when we hear from parents whose children are involved in some aspect of the New Age. One thing you can do as a parent is to cleanse your home, and your child's room, of all objects and items of an unholy nature, such as rock music albums, demonic toys, Satanic posters, idols, and so forth. If you let these remain, you will become accursed of God:

> Neither shall you bring an abomination into thine house lest thou be a cursed thing like it; but thou wilt utterly detest it and thou shalt utterly abhor it, for it is a cursed thing. (Deut. 7:26)

Strengthen your prayer life as well, for prayer is the key that will unlock the door of God's blessings. Always pray each day that God will erect an unsurmountable hedge of protection around your children.

Know and Heed the Signs of Satanic Involvement

Also, you need to know the *warning signs of Satanic involvement* so you can take quick corrective and remedial action if necessary with your own child, or perhaps the child of a neighbor, relative or friend. Please don't wait until it is too late. *Heed the signs.*

The 20 Warning Signs of Satanism

1. A sudden or rapid change in attitude toward authorities.

2. A rebellious, sullen spirit toward parents.

3. Possession or intense interest in occult and magical books. (The possession of the Satanic Bible or a similar book on rituals is of special importance.)

4. A philosophy or attitude that shows a reversal of norms; for example, bad is good and good is bad.

5. Animosity and cynicism towards Christianity, including God, Jesus Christ, the Bible, the church, pastors and youth leaders, and Christian ideals and ethics.

6. Severe mood swings, a drop in grades, intense introspection, depression, loss of sleep, frequent nightmares, paranoia or excessive fear, restlessness.

7. Possession of specific Satanism-related items, which might include knives (especially daggers and knives with bizarre or medieval handles and blades), small pots, cauldrons, or incense burners; special salts or herbs; bells or gongs; tribal drums; animal parts; bones; candles; incense; amulets; talismans; charms.

8. Intense interest in, study of, or dabbling in New Age philosophies, practices, and rituals, such as ESP powers, spirit channeling, crystals, acupuncture, reflexology, reincarnation and karma, etc.

9. Morbid fascination with the dead or with death.

10. Self-mutilation, including cutting oneself or marking with tattoos or body paint.

11. Black colored clothing, when worn almost exclusively, or when combined with the wearing of jewelry, buttons, or paraphernalia with occult symbology. Also, the wearing of such jewelry and paraphernalia with any clothing, T-shirts with pictures of heavy metal album covers or Satanic symbols, and black fingernail polish.

12. Intense interest in heavy metal rock music, including the worship or admiration of rock stars and the hanging of posters of these stars and their albums. Also, interest in New Age "mood" music.

13. Use of illegal drugs of any kind, or alcohol abuse.

14. Obsession with fantasy role-playing games, such as Dungeons & Dragons.

15. Unusual body movements and effects such as twitching, tics, rocking, glazed eyes, head banging, moaning or groaning, chanting.

16. Lack of empathy toward the hurts in other people's lives.

17. Cruelty or inhumane acts against people and animals, or acts of vandalism.

18. Fascination or obsession with horror, slasher and occult movies, or with occult symbols.

19. Use of Satanic nicknames.

20. Fascination with blood.

* * * * *

Please keep in mind that these are *warning signs* of Satanic involvement. However, many teenagers may exhibit some of these behaviors but not be heavily involved in Satanism. They may be dabblers. This, too, is dangerous and often leads to deeper involvement. The more of these warning signs apparent in the child's life, or the higher the intensity, the greater the extent of involvement.

Satan's Big Lie: The Suicide Solution

Satan's objective is to totally destroy your child. The goal is, first, to separate your teenager from Jesus Christ, then, to kill him or her, so that he, Satan, can have the teenager in hell. Thus, Satan attempts to convince young people that *suicide* is the solution to their problems. He will even suggest to them that they will be subsequently rewarded by *him* if they will commit suicide. The warning signs of Satanic involvement therefore are also warning signs of potential suicides. So, please, please, when the warning signs are there, seek God's help through prayer, and take immediate corrective actions to help rid your child of the evil influences.

Seven Steps to Overcoming Occultism and Satanic Involvement

Parents who discover their children are involved in Satanism should always turn first to God and the promises in His Word. He can and will deliver our children from evil. For the young person involved, these seven rules are cardinal steps in eradicating all traces of Satanic influence:

1. Confess your involvement.

2. Break the contact--and contract--with evil. (Renounce your involvement by first identifying each and every act or behavior, then stating aloud to God that you permanently renounce and cast away from your life anything connected with Satan.)

3. Get rid of *all* Satanic articles and items.

4. Ask our Lord Jesus Christ to forgive you and wash you clean of *all* the sins in your life.

5. Acknowledge to God verbally that *He is* your deliverer. Praise Him for your deliverance.

6. Pledge to obey God, to read your Bible, to pray frequently, and witness to others.

7. Stand daily against Satan, always with the full assurance that God *is* almighty and that His strength is always sufficient. Lean on God and He will protect, inspire, and lead you to victory in all things.

Have Courage

Finally, let us as parents, children and teenagers have courage and keep our joy in the Lord Jesus Christ. He was victorious on the cross almost 2000 years ago. *We are on the side that won!*

How can we acquire greater courage when burdens, cares, and fears come into our lives? The answer is to, first, submit yourself to God. Humble yourself, ask forgiveness for sins, ask for strength and joy, and He will do it! He will also intercede for us and put the devil to flight:

Submit yourselves therefore to God. Resist the devil and he will flee from you. Draw nigh to God, and He will draw nigh to you. Cleanse your hands, ye sinners, and purify your hearts, ye double-minded. Be afflicted and mourn, and weep: let your laughter be turned to mourning, and your joy to heaviness. Humble yourselves in the sight of the Lord, and He will lift you up.

(James 4:7-10)

There is power, then, in going to God with a heaviness of heart, with a burden for our kids, afflicted in soul and weeping, and in humbleness. Then, the miracle will occur! He *will* lift you up into heavenly places. He *will* protect your children. He will turn your heaviness into lightness. He will give you joy--Real Joy!

Notes

CHAPTER 1: The Hellish Blueprint for the New Age Assault on Our Children

1. See Joseph Carr, *The Twisted Cross* (LaFayette, LA: Huntington House, 1984).
2. Sir John R. Sinclair, *The Alice Bailey Inheritance* (Wellingborough, Northamptonshire: Turnstone Press Limited, 1984).
3. Alice Bailey (Djwahl Khul), *Education in the New Age* (New York: Lucis Trust, 1954).
4. *Ibid.*, pp. vi-viii.
5. *Ibid.*, pp. 47-48.
6. *Ibid.*, p. 91.
7. *Ibid.*, pp. viii-ix.
8. *Ibid.*, p. 131.
9. *Ibid.*, pp. 111-112.
10. *Ibid.*, p. 112.
11. *Ibid.*, p. 130.
12. *Ibid.*
13. *Ibid.*
14. *Ibid.*, p. 138.
15. *Ibid.*, p. 137.
16. *Ibid.*, p. 77.
17. *Ibid.*, p. 88.
18. *Ibid.*
19. Alice Bailey (Djwahl Khul), *The Reappearance of the Christ* (New York: Lucis Trust, 1948).
20. *Ibid.*, pp. 146-146.
21. *Ibid.*
22. *Ibid.*, pp. 140, 149.
23. *Ibid.*
24. *Ibid.*, pp. 158-159.
25. Alexander Hislop, *The Two Babylons* (New York: Loizeaux, 1959). Also see Ralph Woodrow, *Babylon Mystery Religion* (Riverside, California: Ralph Woodrow Evangelistic Association, 1981).
26. Marilyn Ferguson, *The Aquarian Conspiracy* (Los Angeles, California: J. P. Tarcher, Inc., 1980).
27. *Ibid.*
28. Alice A. Bailey, *The Unfinished Autobiography* (New York: Lucis Trust Publishing, 1951), p. 230.
29. *Ibid.*, p. 50.
30. Alice Bailey (Djwhal Khul), *Esoteric Psychology II* (New York: Lucis Trust Publishing, 1970), p. 282.
31. Sir John R. Sinclair, *The Alice Bailey Inheritance*, p. 124.
32. David Spangler, *Revelation: The Birth of a New Age* (Middleton, Wisconsin: Lorian Press, 1976), p. 24.

CHAPTER 2: From the Womb and Cradle to the Grave

1. Joshua Halpern, *Children of the Dawn: Visions of the New Family* (Bodega, California: Only With Love Publications, 1986).
2. *Ibid.*, pp. 40-41.
3. *Ibid.*, p. 25.
4. *Ibid.*, p. 45.
5. *Ibid.*
6. Sue Browder, *The New Age Baby Name Book* (New York: Warner Books, 1974).
7. *Ibid.*, p. 25.
8. *Ibid.*, p. 27-28.
9. *Ibid.*
10. Shirley Clement and Virginia Field, *Beginning the Search* (Virginia Beach, Virginia: A.R.E. Press, 1978), p. v.
11. *Ibid.*, p. 5.
12. *Ibid.*, p. 7.
13. *Ibid.*, p. 12.
14. *Ibid.*, p. 63.
15. *Ibid.*, p. 68.
16. *Ibid.*, p. 69.
17. *Ibid.*, p. 76.
18. Reda Lucy, *The Lord's Prayer for Children* (Marina del Rey, California: DeVorss & Co., Publisher: 1981).
19. *Ibid.*, p. 5.
20. *Ibid.*
21. Shirley Clement and Virginia Field, *Beginning the Search* (Virginia Beach, Virginia: A.R.E. Press, 1978).
22. *Ibid.*
23. Neil Douglas-Klotz, "The Lord's Prayer: A Creation-Centered Translation," *Creation*, January/February, 1988.
24. *Ibid.*, p. 39.
25. *Ibid.*, p. 40.
26. *CIB Bulletin*, 1988.
27. *Yoga Journal*, November/December, 1988. p. 4.
28. Edmond Harold, *Focus on Crystals* (New York: Ballantine Books, 1986), pp. 22-25.
29. Marilyn Ferguson, *The Aquarian Conspiracy*.
30. *Ibid.*
31. John Bryant, "Educator Criticizes 'Just Say No' Ploy," *Austin American-Statesman*, February 26, 1987.
32. "Getting High On Ecstasy," *Newsweek*, April 15, 1985, p. 96.
33. *Ibid.*
34. *Ibid.*

CHAPTER 3: Girl Scouts, Boy Scouts, Walt Disney, and the YWCA: The Shocking Growth of the New Age Conspiracy

1. *Captain EO*, Walt Disney, produced by George Lucas.
2. *The Disneyland Collections*, Fall, 1986, Vol. 5. No. 2.

3. David Tame, *The Secret Power of Music* (Rochester, Vermont: Destiny Books, 1984), p. 292.
4. *Omega Letter*, June, 1988, p. 23 and *The Houston Chronicle*, February 21, 1988.
5. *Ibid.*
6. Utthita Trikonasana, "Extended Three-Angle Pose," *Yoga Journal*, January/February, 1988, p. 25-27. Also see A. C. Swami Prabhupada, *The Perfection of Yoga* (New York and Bombay: The Bhaktivedenta Book Trust, 1972).
7. George Feurstein, *Yoga Journal*, January/February, 1988, p. 70.
8. *Ibid.*
9. *Girl Scout Handbook*, "Managing Stress," pp. 27-29.
10. *Ibid.*
11. Informational material, Planetary Congress, Toronto, Canada, 1983.
12. Information brochure, Planetary Initiative for the World We Choose.
13. *CIB Bulletin*, February, 1986, also see Appendix to *Earth at Omega*, by Donald Keyes (Branden Press, 1982).
14. Benjamin Ferencz and Ken Keyes, Jr., *Planethood: The Key to Your Survival and Prosperity* (Coos Bay, Oregon: Vision Books, 1st Edition, undated).
15. "Global Understanding," Girl Scouts of America.
16. Global 2000, Interview with William and Penny Bowen, Southwest Radio Church, 1984.
17. Information brochure, Greater Minneapolis Girl Scout Council. Also see *CIB Bulletin*, 1986.
18. *Ibid.*
19. *CIB Bulletin*, 1988.
20. *Ibid.*
21. Ron Zemke, "What's New in the New Age?," *Training Magazine*, September, 1987, pp. 25-33.
22. *CIB Bulletin*, November, 1988, p. 4.
23. *Austin American-Statesman*, November 24, 1988, p. A4.
24. "Is Jesus the Only Way?," *International Christian Digest*, 1987.

CHAPTER 4: First, You Destroy Their Faith in Jesus

1. Jenny Dent, *The Spiritual Teaching for Children Series* (New Lands, England: White Eagle Publishing Trust, 1982), Volumes 1-4.
2. *Ibid.*, Volume 1, introduction.
3. *Ibid.*
4. *Ibid.*, Volume 1, p. 7.
5. *Ibid.*, p. 8.
6. *Ibid.*, p. 9.
7. *Ibid.*, p. 8.
8. *Ibid.*, p. 12.
9. *Ibid.*, Volume 2, p. 4.
10. *Ibid.*, p. 8.
11. *Ibid.*, Volume 3, p. 8.
12. *Ibid.*
13. "Reincarnation Belief Cited in Boy's Burning," *The Daily Oklahoman*, January 22, 1988.
14. *Ibid.*

15. Jenny Dent, Volume 3, p. 9.
16. *Ibid.*, p. 14.
17. *Ibid.*
18. *Ibid.*
19. *Ibid.*, Volume 4, p. 8.
20. *Ibid.*, p. 9.
21. *Ibid.*
22. *Ibid.*, p. 6.
23. *Ibid.*, p. 16.
24. *Ibid.*
25. *Ibid.*, p. 17.
26. *Ibid.*, p. 18.
27. Alice Bailey (Djwhal Khul), *Education in the New Age*, p. 70.

CHAPTER 5: The Ultimate New Age Secret: They Plan to Take Your Children From You

1. Alice Bailey, quoted in "Children: The World's Most Precious Resource," *World Goodwill Newsletter.*
2. *Ibid.*, p. 8.
3. Shree Rajneesh, quoted in *Mystery Mark of the New Age* by Texe Marrs, p. 194 (Westchester, IL: Crossway Books, 1988).
4. Matthew Fox, *The Coming of the Cosmic Christ* (New York: Harper & Row, 1988).
5. *Ibid.*, pp. 27-29.
6. Lola Davis, *Toward a World Religion for the New Age* (Farmingdale, NY: Coleman Publishing, 1983), p. 7.
7. Alice Bailey, "Children: The World's Most Precious Resource," *World Goodwill.*
8. Dr. Frank Alper, *Gabriel's Horn* magazine, Spring, 1988, p. 10.
9. *Ibid.*
10. *Ibid.*
11. Robert Muller, *New Genesis* (Garden City, NY: Doubleday, 1984).
12. Barry McWaters, *Conscious Evolution: Personal and Planetary Transformation* (San Francisco, California: Evolutionary Press, 1982).
13. M. Scott Peck, *A Different Drum: Community Making and Peace* (New York: Simon & Schuster, 1987), p. 17.
14. Lottie Beth Hobbs, "Parental Rights are not Negotiable," *Pro-Family Forum Alert*, January, 1985, p. 3.
15. Ken Wooden, *The Emergence of Ritualistic Crime in Today's Society*, Northern Colorado-Southern Wyoming Detectives Association, September 9-12, 1986, Ft. Collins, Colorado.

CHAPTER 6: This Dark Power That Would Harm a Child

1. Michael Aquino, quoted on the "Oprah Winfrey Show," November 20, 1986.
2. Oprah Winfrey, *Ibid.*
3. Michael Aquino, *Ibid.*
4. Anton LaVey, *The Satanic Bible* (New York: Avon Books, 1969), p. 18.

5. *Ibid.*, pp. 50-51.
6. *Ibid.*, p. 51.
7. *Ibid.*
8. *Ibid.*, p. 96.
9. *Ibid.*, p. 31.
10. *Ibid.*, p. 33.
11. David Spangler, *Reflections of the Christ* (Scotland: Findhorn, 1977), pp. 36-39.
12. *Ibid.*, p. 74.
13. David Spangler, *Revelation: The Birth of a New Age*, p. 36.
14. Benjamin Creme, *The Reappearance of the Christ and the Masters of Wisdom* (London: Tara Press, 1980), p. 95.
15. Sir John R. Sinclair, *The Alice Bailey Inheritance*, and Alice A. Bailey, *The Unfinished Autobiography*, p. 190.
16. Shirley G. Clement and Virginia Fields, *Beginning the Search*, pp. 60-62.
17. Dane Rudhyar, *Occult Preparations for the New Age* (Wheaton, Illinois: The Theosophical Publishing House, 1975), p. 21.
18. *Ibid.*, p. 188.
19. *Ibid.*
20. Vera Alder, *The Initiation of the World* (York Beach, Maine: Samuel Weiser, Inc., 1972), p. 54.
21. *Ibid.*, p. 109.
22. Alice Bailey (Djwhal Khul), *The Rays and the Initiations* (New York: Lucis Publishing Co., 1960).
23. J. Z. Knight, Interview by Paul Zuromski, *Psychic Guide*, Vol. 5, No. 2, December, 1986, pp. 16-18.
24. Jose Arguelles, "Harmonic Convergence, Trigger Event: Implementation and Follow-Up," *Life Times*, Vol. 1, No. 3, pp.63-65.
25. Edouard Schure, *From Sphinx to Christ* (San Francisco, California: Harper & Row, 1982).
26. *Ibid.*, p. 280.
27. *Ibid.*, p. 283.
28. Matthew Fox, *Original Blessing* (Santa Fe, New Mexico: Bear & Company, 1983), p. 213.
29. *Ibid.*, p. 137.
30. *Ibid.*, p. 300.
31. Ralph Metzner, "Owning Our Shadow: Recognizing and Accepting the Enemy Within," *New Realities*, January/February, 1987, pp. 34-37.
32. For example, see Donna Steichen, "The Goddess Comes to Mundelein College," *Fidelity*, September, 1986, pp. 22-31.
33. John Toland, *Adolph Hitler* (New York: Ballantine Books, 1976). Also see Trevor Ravenscroft, *The Spear of Destiny* (York Beach, Maine: Samuel Weiser, Inc., 1973).

CHAPTER 7: The Unholy Childhood of the New Age Child Abusers

1. Bert Wolfe, Introduction to *The Satanic Bible*, by Anton LaVey, p. 11.
2. *Ibid.*, p. 11.

3. Anton LaVey, *The Satanic Bible*, p. 1.
4. David Spangler, *Emergence: The Rebirth of the Sacred* (New York: Delta Books/Dell Publishing, 1984). p. 24.
5. *Ibid.*
6. *Life Times*, Vol 1, Issue No. 3, 1988, p. 23.
7. Chris Griscom, *Ecstasy is a New Frequency* (Santa Fe, New Mexico: Bear & Company, 1987), pp. 124-125.
8. Alice Braemer, *Cultism to Charisma: My Seven Years with Jeanne Dixon* (Smithtown, New York: Exposition Press, 1977).
9. Marilyn Ferguson, quoted in *The Great Transformation* (Bethesda, Maryland: World Future Society, 1983).
10. *Ibid.*
11. Gloria Steinem, quoted in *The Child Abuse Industry* by Mary Pride (Westchester, Illinois: Crossway Books, 1986).
12. "UNICEF: Caring for the World's Children," *World Goodwill News letter*, Vol. 4, 1987, p. 1.
13. Alice Bailey, *Education in the New Age*, p. 89.
14. *Ibid.*
15. Tara Singh, *How to Raise a Child of God* (Los Angeles, California: Life Action Press). Also see Singh's audio tapes, "Raising a Child for the New Age," and "Do Only That: Exploring a Course in Miracles."
16. Robert Muller, *The New Genesis*, p. 155.

CHAPTER 8: *The Great Brain Robbery: The New Age Seduction of America's Classrooms*

1. Virginia Essene, *New Teachings for an Awakening Humanity* (Santa Clara, California: Spiritual Education Endeavors Publishing Company, 1986), pp. 162-163.
2. Gay Hendricks and Russell Wills, *The Centering Book* (New York: Prentice Hall, 1975), pp. 169-170.
3. For example, see Maria Montessori, *To Educate the Human Potential* (Madrid, India: Kalakshetra Publications, 1948); and see the following books by Maria Montessori: *The Three Lords of Ascent, Education for a New World, The Formation of Man,* and *Pedagogical Anthropology*. Also see Elizabeth Hainstock, *The Essential Montessori*, (New York: New American Library, 1978), especially pages 11, 16, 17, 69, 71, 96, 263-285, 302, 323. In addition, see the following: *Montessori Psychology*, Dallas, Texas, Montessori Elementary School Program; and *The Study of History*, Centro Internazionale Di Study Montessoriani, International Center for Montessori Studies. Finally, see the biography, *Maria Montessori*, by Rita Kramer (Reading, Massachusetts: Addison-Wesley Publishing Company, 1988).
4. Elizabeth Hainstock, *The Essential Montessori*, p. 16.
5. *Ibid.* Also see Rita Kramer, *Maria Montessori.*
6. Jane D. Gumprecht, M. D., *Holistic Health: A Medical and Biblical Critique of New Age Deception* (Moscow, Idaho: Ransom Press, 1986), p. 202. Dr. Gumprecht has revised this excellent book which exposes New Age health care practices and the deception of holistic health. The revised title is *New Age Health Care: Holy or Holistic?* (Los Angeles, California; Promise Publishing, 1988).

7. Alice Renton, "Montessori and Cultural Diversity," *The Namta Journal,* Vol. 14, No. 1, Fall-Winter, 1988, pp. 18-19.
8. *Ibid.*
9. *Ibid.,* p. 19.
10. *Ibid.*
11. *Ibid.,* p. 20.
12. Dennis L. Cuddy, "The Trouble With Teaching About Religion," *The News and Observer,* Raleigh, NC, January, 1989, p. 15-A.
13. Oliver L. Reiser, quoted in Alice Bailey, *Education in the New Age,* pp. vi-vii.
14. Alice Bailey, *Education in the New Age,* p. 10.
15. *Ibid.,* p. 14.
16. Vera Alder, *When Humanity Comes of Age* (New York: Samuel Weiser, 1974).
17. Alice Bailey, *Education in the New Age,* pp. 71-73.
18. *Ibid.,* p. 74.
19. Vera Alder, *When Humanity Comes of Age,* p. 72.

CHAPTER 9: *Sex and Sorcery: The Incredible Comic Book Horror Show*

1. *The Gargoyle,* Vol. 1, #3, Marvel Comics, August 1985, pp. 11-15.
2. *Ibid.,* p. 15.
3. *Ibid.,* p. 17.
4. "The Church of Blood," *Who's Who Update,* Vol. 2, DC Comics, 1987, p. 6.
5. *West Coast Avengers,* Marvel Comics, July 1987, p. 17.
6. *Millennium,* DC Comics, Week 8, p. 7.
7. *Ibid.,* pp. 2, 3.
8. "Ghostly Prelude to Armageddon," *The Warlord,* #132, DC Comics, p. 1.
9. *Superman,* #431, DC Comics.
10. *The Ghost Rider,* Vol. 1, #66, Marvel Comics, March 1982.
11. *Arion, Lord of Atlantis,* #26, DC Comics, p. 17.
12. *Ms. Mystic,* origin issue #1, Continuity Comics, pp. 25-26.
13. *Red Sonja,* Vol. 2, #2, Marvel Comics, March 1983.
14. *Johnni Thunder,* Vol. #1, DC Comics, 1984.

CHAPTER 10: *Satan's Bookshelf: Dark Verses, Underground Rhymes, and Bed-Time Stories for Little Witches*

1. *San Jose Mercury News,* July 12, 1986, p. 150; and July 8, 1986, pp. B1, 2.
2. *Ibid.*
3. *Ibid.*
4. *Ibid.*
5. "More Controversy Over Witches," *Education Reporter,* Nov. 1988, p. 2.
6. *Ibid.*

7. Deborah Hautzig, *Little Witch's Big Night* (New York: Random House, 1984).
8. Eva Ibbotson, *Which Witch?* (New York: Scholastic, 1988).
9. *Ibid.,* p. 173.
10. Linda Gondosch, *The Witches of Hopper Street* (New York: Pocket Books, 1986).
11. Zilpha Snyder, *The Egypt Game* (New York: Dell Publishing, 1986).
12. Andrea Packard, *Secret of the Sun God* (New York: Bantam, 1987).
13. Susan Fromberg, *The Dragons of North Chittendon* (New York: Little Simon/Simon & Schuster, 1986).
14. C. S. Lewis, *The Last Battle* (*Chronicles of Narnia* series).
15. *Eternity,* July/August 1988, p. 38.
16. Madeleine L'Engle, *A Cry Like A Bell* (Harold Shaw Publishers, 1987).
17. *Ibid.*
18. *Ibid.*
19. *The Wittenberg Door,* 1987, p. 23.
20. *Ibid.,* p. 24.
21. *Ibid.,* p. 25.
22. Carol Howard, "Bikes Fly for a Course in Campaign," *Austin American-Statesman,* Oct. 11., 1988, p. D-4.
23. *Ibid.*
24. Walt Disney's "The Sorcerer's Apprentice" (New York: Random House, 1973).
25. *Ibid.*
26. Reprinted by columnist Ann Landers, who commented in her column that, in her opinion, it is unacceptable for youth, *Fort Wayne Journal-Gazette,* July 15, 1988.
27. Article by Warren L. McFerran, *The New American,* January 19, 1987, pp. 41, 42.

CHAPTER 11: "Mighty Mouse Snorts Cocaine!"--Hey Kids, It's Show Time!

1. "Jason Motive," *USA Today,* December 1, 1988, p. 3A.
2. "Man Found Guilty of Hatchet Slayings," *Austin American-Statesman,* February 8, 1987.
3. "Topic: Teenage Killers," *USA Today,* November 9, 1987, p. 13A.
4. "Babies Can Learn From TV, study says," *New York Times Service,* December 2, 1988.
5. Study by Louis Harris & Associates. (See the *Omega-Letter,* May, 1988, p. 4).
6. Gene Roddenberry, "Letters to the Next Generation," *Time* magazine, April, 1988. Also see "Startrek: The Next Generation," *USA Today,* October 28, 1987.
7. *The Muppet Show,* as discussed by James Randi in his book, *Flim Flam: Psychics, ESP, Unicorns and Other Delusions* (Buffalo, New York: Prometheus Books, 1986), p. 93.
8. *Ibid.*
9. "A Marriage Made on Sesame Street," *USA Today,* May 12, 1988, p. 3D.
10. "The World's Most Precious Resource: It's Children," *World Goodwill,* New York, pp. 26-27.

11. *Ibid.*
12. Karen Glueck, "Father Andre," (*Life Times,* Vol. 1, No. 4, 1988).
13. Sioux Rose, "Film Media: Oracle of Hope in the Age of Technology," *Psychic Journal* (February, 1988, pp. 47-49).
14. *Ibid.,* pp. 48-49.
15. *Ibid.,* p. 49.
16. *Ibid.*
17. *Ibid.*
18. "CBS' Mighty Mouse Sniffing Cocaine?" *AFA Journal,* July, 1988, p. 4.
19. *Ibid.* Also see *Pathway News* newsletter, Murfreesboro, Tennessee, September, 1988, p. 2; and "CBS Continues Cover-Up in Mighty Mouse Cocaine Scene," *AFA Journal,* August, 1988, p. 1, 23.
20. "CBS' Mighty Mouse Sniffing Cocaine?", *Ibid.*
21. *Ibid.*
22. *West 57th Street,* CBS, January 7, 1989.
23. "ABC Takes Bible Stories to TV With New Series," *Religious Broadcasting,* February, 1987, p. 68.
24. *Ibid.*
25. Stuart Wilde, *The Force* (Taos, New Mexico: Wisdom Books, 1984), p. 2.
26. *Ibid.,* p. 55.

CHAPTER 12: *Toys That Tarnish, Games That Terrorize: The Awful Truth About Dungeons & Dragons, Nintendo and other Occult Adventures*

1. Alexander Hislop, *The Two Babylons* (Neptune, New Jersey: Loizeaux Brothers, 2d American Edition 1959).
2. Phil Phillips, *Turmoil in the Toybox* (Lancaster, Pennsylvania, Star-burst Publishers, 1986).
3. Josephine Bradley, *In Pursuit of the Unicorn* (Corte Madera, California: 1980), pp. 51, 58, 59. Also see Odell Shepard, *The Lore of the Unicorn,* (New York: Harper & Row, 1979).

CHAPTER 13: *Teens Trip Out on Satan: The Rise of Hard-Core Devil Worship and Witchcraft Among Our Youth*

1. David St. Clair, *Say You Love Satan* (New York: Dell Books, 1987).
2. *Ibid.*
3. David Tame, *The Secret Power of Music,* pp. 268, 270, 271.
4. Patrick J. Harbula, "Sounds of Transformation: A Talk With Brother Charles," *Meditation,* Fall 1987, p. 20.
5. *Ibid.,* p. 21.
6. Jack Roper (C.A.R.I.S.), *Analyzing Occult Activity Supplement,* August 1988 Update.

About the Author

Texe Marrs, president of Living Truth Ministries and the Association to Rescue Kids (ARK), in Austin, Texas, has thoroughly researched Bible prophecy, the New Age Movement, and the occult challenge to Christianity. Author of the #1 bestseller *DARK SECRETS OF THE NEW AGE*, and *MYSTERY MARK OF THE NEW AGE*, Texe is a firm believer in the inerrancy of the Bible and salvation through Jesus Christ.

Prior to answering a call to the ministry, Texe was a high-tech consultant and successful author of eighteen books on robotics, computers, and related topics for such major publishers as Simon & Schuster, Dow Jones-Irwin, John Wiley, and Stein and Day. Previous to that, he was a career officer in the U.S. Air Force. For five years he was assistant professor of aerospace studies at the University of Texas at Austin, and he has taught international affairs, political science, and American Government for two other universities. Texe graduated summa cum laude from Park College in Kansas City, and earned his Master's degree at North Carolina State Univesrity.

Texe Marrs is internationally recognized as the foremost authority on New Age cults and religions. He and his wife, Wanda, who is herself actively involved in the ministry, frequently appear on radio and TV interviews across America.

For More Information

Texe Marrs and Living Truth Ministries offer a free newsletter about Bible prophecy, the New Age Movement, cults, the occult challenge to Christianity, our children and other important topics. If you would like to receive this newsletter, please write to:

Texe Marrs
Living Truth Ministries
8104 Shiloh Court
Austin, TX 78745

Also by Texe Marrs

BOOKS

MYSTERY MARK OF THE NEW AGE: Satan's Design for World Domination
DARK SECRETS OF THE NEW AGE: Satan's Plan for a One World Religion
MEGA FORCES: Signs and Wonders of the Coming Chaos

VIDEOS

TEXE MARRS EXPOSES SATAN'S NEW AGE PLAN FOR A ONE WORLD ORDER:
  Is the Reign of Antichrist Just Ahead?

TAPES

NIGHT COMETH!
  The New Age Beast and His Riders of Death
NIGHTSOUNDS:
  The Hidden Dangers of New Age music